Old Memories

Sir HENRY JONES, C.H.

First published and printed in
Great Britain
by William Lewis (Printers), Ltd., *Cardiff,*
c.1923

This edition
published in Wales in 2002 by
the Trustees of the Sir Henry Jones
Memorial Trust
and
Conwy County Borough Council

ISBN 1-84047-006-2

Printed and bound by
Bridge Books
Wrexham

Preface

Sir Henry Jones's Old Memories has long been out of print, and it is with great pleasure that the Trustees of the Sir Henry Jones Memorial Trust and Conwy County Borough Council issue this reprint to mark the one hundred and fiftieth anniversary of his birth. Sir Henry Jones occupied a position of great eminence in public life as a philosopher and educationalist from his appointment to the Chair of Philosophy at Bangor in 1884 to his death in Scotland in 1922. During his career he was appointed to three professorships, awarded two doctorates, elected a Fellow of the Royal Academy, awarded the gold medal of the Honourable Society of Cymmrodorion, made a knight, and chosen by the king to be a Companion of Honour.

Sir Henry was born in 1852, the son of a village shoemaker, in the (then) Denbighshire village of Llangernyw. Throughout his long and distinguished career, much of it pursued beyond the borders of his native Wales, he frequently acknowledged his indebtedness to the values instilled in him as a boy and youth by the community in which he was raised. He himself played a prominent role in the evolution of Welsh secondary and university education during the closing decades of the nineteenth century.

His zeal for the promotion of education in Wales was born of his own mighty struggles to acquire an education himself as a young man. The vividness of his account of that struggle in *Old Memories*, together with his finely observed description of rural life in Wales during the second half of the nineteenth century, has secured for it the status of a classic.

Very shortly before he died, Sir Henry handed the manuscript of *Old Memories* to Thomas Jones, a former student of his at Glasgow, who himself rose to a position of great eminence as a public servant and pioneer of adult education. He had been working on it during the last two years of his life as he fought bravely against cancer. Although the original manuscript contained dictated notes on Sir Henry's life as Professor of Moral Philosophy at Glasgow, Thomas Jones felt it was best to exclude these sections from the published work. We concur with him in this, and have for this edition also excluded the treatment of Sir Henry's short period at St. Andrews (chapter 7 of the original book as published). This edition therefore ends with Sir Henry's final departure from Wales in 1891. A memoir which deals with the life of Sir Henry up to his death in 1922 was prepared by another of his eminent former students, H. J. W. Hetherington, *The Life and Letters of Sir Henry Jones* (1924).

Old Memories tells a story which has lost none of its power to stir and inspire, and is now published in the belief that readers in the twenty-first century will still feel moved by it.

On behalf of the Trustees
E. Gwynn Matthews
University of Wales, Bangor.

Illustrations

Dedication

*This book is dedicated to
my beloved wife,
my strength and my peace
during the last forty years.*

Sir Henry Jones, C.H.

Chapter I

I was born, they tell me, on the 30th day of November, 1852, in a little cottage called Cwm, near the small village of Llangernyw, in Denbighshire; and, in order to make as sure as possible of my eternal safety, I was baptized in the village church by the rector of the parish on the same day. My father was the village shoe-maker; not a cobbler, be it noted, whose grade is decisively lower; for my father made new boots as well as mended old ones. My mother, before her marriage, had been servant maid in a succession of farms. She was the prettiest brunette, I was told, in all the country round, and known everywhere for her cleverness and sprightliness.

Better blood than mine could run in no child's veins. It was not blue; but it was red with the healthy redness of simple lives led in the open air. And, so far as I ever heard, there was among my progenitors not a single liar, or coward, or sneak, or lounger, or hard and unkind man. All my ancestors whose story I can trace were either farmers or farm labourers except my father. They followed the plough and the harrow, wielded the scythe and the sickle on the meadows, and habitually welcomed 'the morn in russet mantle clad' over the brow of the neighbouring eastern hill.

My mother, her father and her father's father, and, I believe, my grandmother and great-grandmother also were deeply religious. My great-grandfather and great-grandmother, I think, must have been amongst those earliest dissenters who, in Wales at that time, suffered a good deal of persecution. They lived for a time in the little chapel house at Cefn Coch; and the old lady had charge of keeping the chapel clean, sweeping its floors and dusting its pews, once a week.

They were 'members' of their church, and not merely 'hearers' or 'adherents.' And to be a 'member' of a dissenting church meant a good deal in those days. It meant much more than partaking of the sacrament when the communion was celebrated, and the little, cheap, ordinary, earthenware sacramental cup was passed around, from lip to lip. The 'members' were a select few, who stayed behind for more intimate spiritual communion when the mass of the congregation walked out at the end of the sermon. There was hardly one of them who could not point back to the very day of his conversion, or at least to a period when the sense of sin or the fear of hell, — yielding place sometimes after many weeks of torture to a consciousness of forgiveness, a great peace and a deep joy — overwhelmed the soul. That the conversion was sincere could hardly be doubted, for nothing was to be gained at that time by pretending to be a converted dissenter and much might be lost. Conversion thus meant that those who experienced it had really felt, in some fashion or another, the power of the things of the spirit, and had from that day on dedicated themselves to religion. Their homes were sacred with the daily prayers offered in them morning and evening, and sometimes at midday; and their knowledge of the Bible was marvellous. They read nothing else, of course, and they read it very closely; for was not every word in it 'the word of God'? My grandfather, on my mother's side, could turn at once to any verse you might want, and tell you before hand on what page of his own big Bible it was to be found and whether at the top, middle, or bottom.

I have a fairly distinct memory of this grandfather of mine. His name was William Williams and he died when I was about ten years old. I can yet see him stooping over and leaning hard on the two sticks by the help of which he walked. Above all I remember seeing him on his knees in 'the big pew' of the little chapel, with his head thrown far back and his face turned upwards as he pleaded in passionate earnestness in prayer with his God. I remember him also in the Sunday School which he attended to the end of his life with faithfulness. He was over seventy years of age at the time, and so, I have no doubt, were most if not all of his fellow-scholars in the class. His 'teacher' was a rich old shop-keeper of the name of Robert Roberts. 'I don't know what to do with that old shop-keeper,' grumbled my grandfather one Sunday afternoon after the Sunday school. 'He has been gloating for three Sundays over the chapter that tells of the wealth of Job, wondering what the price of a camel and a yoke of oxen was in those days. I can't get him away from it.' For the Sunday School in Wales is an institution for adults as well as for children; and the sanest of all educational institutions in that respect, for it rests on the assumption that the care of the soul, like the care of the body, should be life-long — an assumption which not even a life spent amongst college dons has been able to disprove. My grandfather lived next door to my father and mother and made walking-sticks in the evenings, while my grandmother stitched and sewed patchwork quilts; and he made presents of the walking-sticks to the most select of his friends. One item more completes his life so far as I remember it. He gave me a lesson in reading Welsh, and, one day, sitting on the side of the bed in my father's workshop, he impressively put on his spectacles, examined the stitches, one by one, which by way of learning to be a shoemaker I had put in a leather patch, and he criticised them, praising here and blaming there, as if he was dealing with a work of high art. He was 'a born teacher.' He was also, most probably, a natural orator, for he was the most beautiful public reader of the Bible in all the country round; and most probably of quite a distinct literary genius. In any case his life was very beautiful; for he was kindly and very playful as well as devout; and he nursed and nurtured his character on the finest book in the world, day by day, throughout the whole of a long, humble, industrious and very peaceful life. During the latter part of his life, and for a great many years he worked on the estate of the squire, Sandbach. When he became old his wages were repeatedly reduced. They were at last reduced to 4s. a week, which was starvation wages even in those days, and on this 4s. a week he was expected to live himself and keep his home going. But the ultimate reward of his long and faithful service was half-a-crown for a week's work; and then, my mother told me, 'he broke his heart.'

Of my grandfather on my father's side I have much less to say. He was the tenant of a small farm, situated near the borders of three parishes, — Llanfair Talhaiarn, Llansannan and Llanefydd. The farm was itself bordered on the one side by a deep, dark, thickly-wooded gully, which was infested at nights with bogies. No one who could help it went through 'Nant-y-Chwil' at, or after, midnight. His name was John Jones, and he was the son of a Harri Jones, a farmer whose descent I cannot trace, except to Adam and Eve. John Jones was a little man, very fond of horses (and horses of him!); and he had a tall wife and nine children, of whom my father, Elias, was the eldest. John Jones died when he was about sixty years old. He was ploughing in his shirt-sleeves in a shower of rain, got thoroughly wet, and after that put on his jacket. He caught a chill and died of it. His wife, my grandmother, lived after him for many years. She visited us occasionally, and I can always see her knitting and hear her speaking a little in jerky monosyllables. My father never spoke much to me about his parents; but he told me one thing, when he was an old man, and told it with a simple pathos that made his story grip. It was about his mother. Whenever she sent him to stay for a week or two at his grandfather's farm, she gave him a thoroughly sound thrashing, asking him between the blows 'Will you remember *now* to be a good boy? 'These *before-hand* beatings he could not think quite fair.

The strain, the disposition, the temperament, the character, the whole outlook on life and the way of living it, of the sides of my parentage were distinctly different. On the one side the whole make and bent of the soul, its natural tendencies and its history, were of the religious type. There was intuition, passion, yearning after perfection, imagination of what the best might be, and the pursuit of it; and the soul was so dedicated to the things 'beyond,' that this life, with its opportunities and chances and even ethical obligations, was in the background. On my father's side, on the other hand, we had the thoroughly secular but also thoroughly moral spirit. Honesty, simplicity, industry, truthfulness, fidelity, and above all an abounding neighbourliness and kindliness, were the ruling powers. A 'slack' job never passed through my father's hands, or through those of any of his eight brothers and sisters. I adore his memory; and I will not promise what I cannot perform, namely, to speak of him in measured terms. My mother was religious. Her mind had an imaginative reach which my father's had not; and if ever man or woman was endowed with that kind of intuitive power which, psychologists say, reaches true conclusions without the help of any premises, it was my mother. She also like her father knew her Bible well, and how to use its verses — sometimes for dreadful castigation and reproof; she read any and every novel (in Welsh) that came within her reach; and she attended

Elias and Elizabeth Jones, the parents of Sir Henry Jones.

every sermon and marked every poetic turn it might take. My mother was imaginative and aesthetic and intuitive to the finger-tips; and she was extraordinarily clever.

My parents, between them, gave to me and to my two older brothers and my single sister, a first-rate up-bringing. I should not be exaggerating much if I said that my mother, when I was a boy between six or seven and thirteen, thumped me out of the house and into the open air, with a piece of bread-and-butter in my hand, every day of my life — taking care, however, never really to hurt. We were all habitually turned out of the house to play in the open air when it was 'not raining'; and if it was raining we had our games in the bake-house, which was under the same roof as our own and our grandmother's cottage, and which being doorless was by no means air-less. In the daytime, of course, we were in school, except at meals; and in the evenings we were in the little chapel close by, where there was some service or another every night of the week — except Saturdays.

Decisively, there was no room for us all in my father's house, or at least no room for us to move about, or do anything. It consisted of one room downstairs measuring about ten feet each way, and a room of the same size and shape upstairs. The ceiling was about six feet high with its white-washed rafters. The window of the room upstairs was kept open — a rare thing for cottagers at that time but one of my mother's sane fads. The window of the room in which we lived, where all the cooking was done and the meals eaten and the visitors entertained — kitchen, dining-room, drawing-room, living room all in one — was never opened. It was half blocked with geraniums, and there hung in front of it a bird's cage with a much-made of goldfinch hopping about and singing inside. So far as sleeping-room was concerned we fared not so badly; for my eldest brother William and I slept — slept and quarrelled — in one of our grandmother's beds next door.

This house was my real 'home', the only 'home' I had till I found one of my own. But I was not born in it. I was born in a low, long, thatched, small-windowed, very old-fashioned house at the foot of a little hill close by. My parents moved from it when I was six months old, and every vestige of it has disappeared long ago. I wish I could describe its spacious hearth, with room for fire-place and oven, and chimney-bench (*maingc y simnai*), seated on which neighbours were entertained, and songs were sung and tales of ghosts were told. If you looked up through the great open chimney you would. see a wide expanse of sky overhead. If you looked into the room — the kitchen — you would find it rich with flitches of bacon, and very ill-lit by the petty window in front and still smaller one at the back. At the other end was the ground-floor bed-room, and on the other side of the bed-room wall was the barn. Attached to the barn again was a small cow-house, with its gable against a slight slope, on the top of which, looking down at the cow-house, was my father's workshop, — a 'lean-to,' attached to my real 'home'.

I have a distinct memory of this old thatched house, and of some of its tenants. Even yet I can hear the thump, thump, thump of the flail, and the fourth gentler thump, as it was swung three times to the left and once to the right, all day long, to thresh the corn grown on the little farm. The threshing, now done in a few hours by a visiting 'fire-engine', then occupied the farm labourer all the wet days of the winter and occupied him very peacefully. I also remember the excitement of seeing a new calf in the byre, and its being fed; so that it was there that, one way or another, I got my first experience of a wider world.

Returning now to my proper home, I cannot but marvel at the skill that secured its comfort for all of us. A happier household, I believe, there never was; and though my father, I should say, never made a pound a week, we never lacked anything, so far as I could see, whether in the way of wholesome food or of comfortable and respectable clothing. Of course it is not possible to make the 'plenty' of a good working man's home intelligible to the well-to-do. Things which look like impossibilities are achieved every day; and the so-called Laws of Domestic Economy are abstract generalities compared with the concrete sense and skill of the clever mother. Let me illustrate. Seven persons had all their meals every day in that little ten-foot kitchen, where the food was cooked and the family lived. There was no room for us all to sit at our table; neither the table nor the room was big enough. What then? The answer is simple; we took our meals in relays. First came my two elder brothers, both of them apprentice gardeners at the squire's (on terms, I may say in passing, which though possibly common enough in those days, now seem to me to have been villainously hard: for the apprenticeship to common gardening lasted for seven years; and the wage began at 4s. a week, was increased by 1s. each year, and culminated in 10s. a week). My brothers generally arrived home at mid-day ravenously hungry: for they had had a most hasty breakfast, owing to unfailingly 'sleeping in,' and they had dug and delved all the morning in the open air. Their food was, perhaps by some trifle, a little better, or better served, than what followed. After them came my father, bringing his princely good-nature and unselfishness and splendid appetite; and with him came one (or sometimes two) of his workmen. What meal I had I generally took standing, being always in a hurry to go out to play. When my younger sister fed I cannot remember; but everything that concerned her was 'special.' My mother sat at peace to her dinner later on, after she had attended to all our needs, and she ate it at leisure. On Sundays, when we had fresh meat, we all dined at the same time, one, or perhaps two of us, sitting on the doorstep if the weather was fine, with the plate on our knees. But neither on Sunday nor on week-day was the meal scanty, or the fun and chatter lean, or was there any faintest hint of scarcity or poverty.

Let me give another example. There was no room for the cradle in the day-time on that crowded ten-foot floor, when my second, little, short-lived sister was born. What was to be done? Well! the cradle was put upstairs, a string was let down from it through a hole in the low ceiling, and whenever the baby cried my mother bade one of us pull the string. I can hear the rick-rock of the cradle above my head even yet, when I sit down to listen to old memories.

As to the clothing matters were just as easy. I don't think mother ever had or needed anything new; but she adorned everything she wore when she was 'dressed.' My father never had new Sunday clothing so far as I ever heard; but the tailor had to come, say about once a year, and, sitting with his apprentice on our kitchen table, make him a new pair of strong, ribbed, everyday breeches. What other new clothes were made went, naturally, to my elder brothers. The clothes that became too small for them were made down to me. I think I was more than sixteen years old when I had my first new jacket; and I know that when I sat for the Queen's Scholarship, in Bangor, at eighteen years of age, I had the loan of the suit of clothes of one brother in order that I might look respectable, and the loan of the watch of the other brother in order that I might 'time' the answers to the questions. No indignity was meant; none was ever thought of. We were all partners in one family enterprise, and all things ran smoothly in their course.

Our food was somewhat monotonous, and possibly we might have done better with less buttermilk and more sweet-milk. But, while the latter was plentiful and cheap and good, the former was to be had in big can-fulls for the mere fetching. It was the customary return made by our neighbours for some kindly deed or another of my father's or mother's. On the whole the victualling was as wholesome as it was plentiful. It consisted of bread-and-milk or of 'shot,' that is, ground oat-cake and milk, or of bread and soup — the soup made out of dripping bought at the squire's hall, being, I under stand, the cook's perquisite. And the bread was of my mother's own making — the best in all the land! Even yet I think that no bread can rival the big loaves turned out of the domestic ovens of Wales and Brittany.

Such was our home, and our daily life in it. It was crowded and restless, with something going on at every moment. Either my mother was cooking, or my father was heating his polishing irons in the kitchen fire, or some of us children were clamouring for bread-and-butter, or a neighbour had stepped in to find if his boots were ready or to enjoy a chat. But we helped, and I think I may say, we inspired each other; and we were very happy.

A better-fitted pair than my father and mother there could hardly be. She ruled always in little things, and my father's attitude towards her was obviously idolatrous, and charming to witness. Hers to him was mischievous to the last degree, and his patience occasionally gave way for brief moments. Then he would grumble, and endure and join in the fun. 'Be about to-night, Harry! when your father is going to bed,' she said to me one day. I took care to do as I was told, for I knew something was up. My father proceeded to take off his day-shirt: instead of coming over his head, it pulled up his trousers. He tried to pull off his trousers; but found that he was only tightening his shirt at the shoulders. Mother sat by, watching and laughing, and

The home and workshop at Llangernyw.

he knew then that some trick or another had been played on him. He lost his temper just for the moment, as often happened, seized the shirt firmly by the two shoulders and tore out its hold on the trousers. It was then her turn to cry, 'Don't, Elias!' The brace-button had come off during the day, mother had been asked to sew it on again, and she seized the opportunity of making him incapable, as she thought, of undressing himself.

I am tempted to tell another little story. It illustrates so well the atmosphere of our happy home. I was home on a visit, and, I believe, a professor at St. Andrews at the time. I was sitting in the kitchen, the only living-room, chatting with my mother, when my father came in. He had been out, taking his usual evening walk after his day's work, along the quiet country road, and in the dark. 'I think', he said to my mother as he was sitting down, 'I think I have caught two lovers'. 'No!' cried my mother as full of excited interest as if she were a young woman, 'who were they, Elias?' 'I'll not tell you' he replied, 'for you will not believe me.' She begged, and of course, he gave in, bidding me observe that my mother would refuse to believe him. 'It was Robert Davies, the tailor,' he said, 'and Mrs. Roberts, the widow who lives at the chapel house.'

Robert Davies was a serious-minded elder, about sixty-five years old and a widower. 'Don't talk nonsense! 'cried my mother, rejecting his tale just as he had foretold. 'Well,' said he at length, when she persisted in her unbelief, 'I'll tell you what I saw, and you can judge for yourself. As I was passing the door of Mrs. Roberts's house, it was opened and a flood of light poured out. Robert Davies walked in, and I saw him quite plainly. He had a ham under his arm. I lingered about, and in about a quarter of an hour or twenty minutes Robert Davies came out, without the ham. 'Well! well!' cried my mother, her scepticism completely overcome by the evidence of the 'ham', which was evidently, for her as for my father, conclusive proof of marital intentions, if not also of the tender passion. I thought the whole scene between my father and my mother one of the most humorous I had ever witnessed, and felt I had discovered a new use for hams!

Although the contagion of its humour was irresistible on one or two occasions I thought my mother's fondness for making fun of my father carried her too far, despite his charming way, after a helpless little period of anger and grumbling, of taking the joke. It was his habit for many a year to go about once every twelve months to his sister's farm, and have a week of ferreting, of which he was very fond. On one of these occasions, having failed to finish his new flannel shirt, she sent him away in it only tacked together. He had a week of trouble over that shirt, for the tacking gave way, and he came home in what was for him very ill-humour. 'Look here!' he said to my mother, as he took a wrist-band out of one pocket and the collar of his shirt out of another! while he showed how a very rough device of his own kept back and front connected, and held the sleeves at the shoulder. It was really too bad! But it was also overwhelmingly comical, and my mother sank into a chair, with her two hands in her lap, quite overcome with laughter.

What with the mixture of happiness, fun, good health and hard work we did, on the whole, uncommonly well in that humble little house. My eldest brother, William, came out second in the United Kingdom in an examination held by The Society of Arts and Sciences in the subjects of 'Fruit and Vegetable Culture' and 'Floriculture.' My next brother, John, came out easily first in the Kingdom, in a similar examination held some years later by the same society. And at the earliest allowable age, and while still a working shoe-maker, I passed, out of the same noisy and restless little kitchen, into the Normal College for Schoolmasters at Bangor, at the head of the college list, and first in the Kingdom of all the non-pupil teacher candidates.

I pass over the Eisteddfodic prizes we won from time to time: for essays, recitation, singing, reading and so forth. They were insignificant except for the joy they gave my father, who could not help telling, every now and then, how out of one competitive meeting thirteen prizes were won by his boys. It was a good home. For me, at any rate, none could have been better. 'Learning,' of which my father had none, for he had left school when he was seven years old, was held in high esteem. (I remember when I was a big boy, waiting for hours for a B.A. to pass along the road, and then failing, from very reverence, to speak to him.) The respect for learning was due to my father. He would allow nothing to break the regularity of our attendance at the village school. And long before he left the school to become a gardener's apprentice, my eldest brother, 'William Jones — *One*' as he was called by the schoolmaster to distinguish him from William Jones *Two*, was by far the best scholar. There was an interesting and emphatic proof of this fact. William happened to be ill with measles, or scarlet fever (I cannot remember which) when the Diocesan Inspector came to examine the school. The absence of the finest scholar was keenly felt by the teacher, and by Mr. Sandbach, the squire, and, possibly, also by the inspector. So William was sent for. My mother wrapped him in a blanket, my father carried him to the school, the teacher placed him in his class amongst the other children, and William carried off all the prizes. Sanitary regulations were below the horizon at that time.

I am sorry to say that I cannot speak well of the village school, or, at least, of the village schoolmaster. He was very cruel and very ignorant. The cane was in his hand from the opening of the school in the morning to its close at four o'clock in the afternoon: faults, errors, slips, a constant succession of petty nothingnesses led to its use, either on the hand or on the back or on both hands and back. Some child whispers; he cannot find out which. He thrashes the class all round. The answer to the sum is wrong, the boot is not exactly at the chalk line, a child has turned his head round, there are more than a certain number of errors, say three, in the dictation, a lad has spoken in Welsh — any of these might be a reason for a whacking; and there was lamentation in the school all day long. The master had one merit. He was thoroughly energetic. But it would have been better, I believe, had he been lazy and careless, and left the children a lighter burden of care and fear.

But probably what the boys disliked most in him were his obvious favouritisms. These were shown invariably to the well-dressed children of the well-to-do, who attended, not the Methodist or Baptist chapel, but the village church. They were hardly ever caned, even lightly. But the chapel-going children, and especially those who were poor or slow, suffered many a blow, and were stung by many a vulgar sarcasm levelled at their 'religion'.

The picture is not agreeable and I hasten on. Personally, I may say, I suffered comparatively little at the schoolmaster's hands. I was something of a favourite; and a most emphatic distinction was made between me and my brother John who was always being caned, and always unrepentant, and always first favourite on the playground. But I must not forget the master's attitude towards the Welsh language, the only habitual language of the village and country. The speaking of it was strictly forbidden, both in the school and in the playground. The master every morning handed over to a child in each of the higher classes a small block of wood, through which a string passed. That child was to watch and listen till he heard someone speak Welsh: and one Welsh word was enough. Then the 'Welsh stick' was passed on, and every child who held it had either a stroke of the cane, or two verses of the Bible to learn, as a penalty.

I think John must have been very able. He was not so prominent as a scholar as my eldest brother William was — who was easily the best of his time; and I shared John's lessons although he was two and a half years older than I was. But he never gave himself to his lessons as I did: and he had far more ideas and interests of his own. I was naturally his slave; the younger brother always is in 'a well-regulated family', by which I mean a family which is regulated as little as possible and in which the parents interfere only on grave occasions. But I was by no means the only boy who found his guide, philosopher and friend in John, who had a genius for leadership in all 'practical enterprises', such as we considered games.

There was evidence of his ability to lead. Every summer for some years, sometime in June, I believe, when the turnips in the fields of the farmers were sufficiently grown out of the ground, the village school broke up. And a gang, consisting mainly though not merely of boys, went from farm to farm to thin the turnips, receiving first 8d., then 10d., then a shilling a day's wages — fourpence a day being taken off if we had our meals on the farm. The whole of our school holidays, extending for four or five weeks, were spent at this work. I had a few days of it when I was only five-and-a-half years old, my mother — it must have been with too little reflection — letting me go with my bigger brothers. I remember yet the expanse of the time between meals, the length of the day, and my being carried home from Cammaes, too tired to walk, by the bigger boys. From the time I was six-and-a-half years old, till I began shoe-making, I thinned turnips for the farmers every year. John was our gang-man. He assigned to every boy and girl a place in the gang, and made all the arrangements with the farmers; and no autocrat could exercise more unquestioned authority. By this work he and I each made some 25s. to 27s. every summer, sums that were as a matter of course handed over to our mother, and valued by her as substantial helps to her house-keeping.

What my age was when I first attended school I cannot say: probably, about four-and-a-half; for I remember well sitting on the knees of the bigger girls, and being 'mothered' by them. But the incidents which have clung to my mind are very few. I cannot forget the cold feet in the winter, or how we longed, in vain, to get near the fire. Nor can I forget my introduction of a live and wild squirrel into the school, and the commotion and utter confusion it caused as it ran to and fro along the floor, climbed up the children and jumped from one to another, seeking to escape. Moreover, I was singled out to recite, when the school was celebrating the marriage of the Prince of Wales (afterwards King Edward the Seventh). Nor can I forget the incident which I am tempted to call 'the proudest of my life'. Toe-caps had come into fashion. A pair of boots with toe-caps was ordered of my father. The stitching of the toe-cap had to be specially accurate and fine; and my father, when I was a boy of about twelve, came to school to fetch me to do that sewing. There was not in the whole of Great Britain a prouder spirit than mine as I walked at my father's side across the play-ground to do this bit of work.

I left school when I was twelve-and-a-half years old, and put on my little shoe-maker's leather apron: and a new and most happy page of my life was opened. There are few, if any, pleasanter scenes in the world than those presented by the little workshops of the country shoe-makers and tailors. There, master and man sit working side by side, talking freely with one another about anything and everything; for they sit quite near each other, and the strain of the work is not so heavy or constant as to prevent either conversation or singing. Not that the talk was uninterrupted, or that the songs were ever sung right through. On the contrary, I never heard my father or anyone of his workmen sing anything but snatches.

> Hurrah for France and England! Victoria and Napoleon
> Have beaten Alexander: Sebastopol no more.

would suddenly break out during an interval of uncritical work, such as hammering the sole leather on the lap-stone. Then it would break off, and one rarely, if ever, heard any more. This was one of my father's musical outbreaks. Or, perhaps, George, the best (and most drunken) of all my father's workmen, would strike in, when opportunity offered, with

> Nelly Bly shuts her eye, when she goes to sleep.

or with

> The fox and the hare and the badger and the bear,
> And the birds on the greenwood tree,
> And the pretty little rabbits, so engaging in their habits,
> They all have their mates, but me.

Then there were discussions and debates, and the village news had to go round, and my father was always crammed full of mischievous fun and anecdotes.

The discussions and the debates were rarely political, and they were never religious; but some of them would interest and occupy the mind of the workshop, off and on, for days. Above all, there was story-telling and tales of the experiences of other days; and the chief of the story-tellers was my father. Many a time I have heard a neighbour, as he sat on the side of the bed near the head of my father's bench of tools, beg him to repeat some well-known tale. That it had been told the hearer many times before was no reason against telling it again. It was the exact opposite; so thoroughly did my father enjoy the telling, and so contagious was his enjoyment.

Knowing the joys of the workshop as I did, I think it no wonder that I insisted on being allowed to be a shoe-maker, and stubbornly refused to be either a blacksmith (my mother's choice for me), or a joiner, or a grocer's boy, or a gardener, or any other of the crafts urged upon me, as 'better than shoe-making' as a means of a livelihood. I knew, knew in that decisive way which we call 'feeling', that if I made shoes, I could hear and share in what was going on in the workshop; and I could sit side by side with my father whose favourite I was, and whom I adored.

I had two mastering ambitions at that time, both of them at once strong and steady: one was to become a first-rate shoe maker, and the other was to be made an elder in the little Calvinistic Methodist chapel, when I was a man.

Perhaps I ought to try to describe the little workshop where I sat, day by day, for the next five or six years. It was a lean-to at the gable-end of my father's cottage; and its single window looked south — not east like the windows of the house. For a view there was the byre, and the old thatched cottage of which I have already spoken. The window was large, for the size of the room, and it was low, in order that the light might fall on the boots we had making or mending on our knees. My father's seat, with its tools on his right and a little drawer beneath, and also the workman's seat faced this window; and they were placed at such a distance from each other as would permit my father and the workman to stretch their arms in sewing without fear of collision. Behind the workman's seat and near the door was my own, and on the right of mine was that of James Pugh. He was the postman; but he worked at ladies' boots during the interval between his arrival from Llanrwst with the letter bags and his departure back again. Pugh was a most neat workman, minutely careful, but very slow. At the further end of the room, and opposite the door, was the workman's bed. It was most untidy. There were leather skins at the foot of it, and old boots and lasts underneath it: it was the seat, the only seat, for the visitors and it was never 'made'.

There was not much chance of privacy in that little workshop. Practically every thought was shared, sooner or later.

I have no doubt that the air was bad, the place was so small and we were so crowded; but we never felt it except perhaps in the evenings, after dark, when my father, the workman and myself sat round the same penny candle-dip, and our working-men neighbours had leisure to visit us. The air was then felt to be somewhat close.

We worked, as a rule, from 8*a.m.* to 8*p.m.*; but we were apt to work later on Saturdays, for there was always something that had to be 'finished'. But we had an interval for the simple dinner and a very short walk at mid-day; and we had Tea. The 'Tea' was a superb meal. Mother's hand had prepared it and made the toast; and her hand had the magic touch of the born cook's, — like that of the wife of Uncle Tom in *Uncle Tom's Cabin*. And 'Tea' had an excellence of its own. It stopped the yawning and lifted off the listlessness of the afternoons; so that, after tea, we gripped our work with new energy and new joy. Neither did we loosen that grip till the time came when we spread our leather aprons over our tools at the close of the day, and took a good warm-water wash in the open air — for only warm water would take the wax off our hands and only outside was there room to rub our hands and faces. Then we went forth into the evening quiet, each his own way, with his own companion and after his own private interest, and we breathed and enjoyed the fresh air as we went for our long walks along the country roads.

Am I wrong in believing that all this time, amidst such scenes, and sharing in the fun, the discussions and the experience, merry and sad, of such companions, I was receiving a first-rate education? Not, when I recall the depth of its influence upon my after-life, and especially upon my judgment of men and their ways. Not, above all, when I leave plenty of room for my father in the picture.

When I think of him in his relations to me what comes first is his gentleness, and close upon his gentleness came his patience. The boots I made as a learner were, as a matter of course, handed round the workshop at different stages, and turned over and over, and I was praised or blamed or both, just as if we were dealing with works of art. And so we were: for the spirit of art was awake and active in the little country workshops, in those days.

My father reproved me once while I worked at his side. — It was for joining with the company in making fun of him! My repentance was overwhelming, and it is not over even yet. Day after day, with infinite patience, he listened to my chatter and to my incessant questioning as to whether I could pass into college or not. For that adventure, as I shall tell, had appeared above my horizon. His mischief and fondness for fun were inexhaustible; and the boys who took their mid-day dinner of warmed bread and-milk in our house, as they attended school, crowded into the workshop to chat with him. And he told them the most outrageous nonsense — and, above all, addressed them always as grown-up men.

But was there anyone in distress in the neighbourhood? My father was at his side as a matter of course — so much a matter of course that the neighbours as a rule no more thought of thanking him than of thanking the sun for shining. A stranger farmer's boy is squeezed between the shafts of the waggon and the wall. It is my father who watches him dying in the loft above the stable: the farmer is sleeping in his own bed. The news must be gently broken to the boy's mother. My father walks, some thirteen or fourteen miles each way, to Rhyl to tell her. A drunken and surly and little-liked Scottish shepherd dies in his remote cottage. Mother, just to let me see, argues against my father's going to the funeral. When he insisted that there might be no one there to lift the corpse, she replied, 'Well! that is not *your* affair. He has left you sufficiently in the lurch already, for his debts will never be paid'. My father yields for the moment. But the scene is soon repeated; and matters end by my father tossing his leather apron to one side, washing his face, putting on his Sunday clothes, taking his workman with him, and attending the funeral. He returns home very happy: the most beautiful sample of a gentle humanity in all the land.

But the crowning example of the beauty of his character came to my knowledge in quite an incidental way. Our next-door neighbour, a wealthy and most stingy shop-keeper, was dying of consumption. Day after day he sent for my father to sit with him in the parlour and amuse him. It was often difficult for him to go, for someone or another was clamouring for his boots; but he never once refused. On his arrival, the invalid would call out of the parlour to the housekeeper, 'Ellen Owens! bring a chair out of the kitchen for Elias Jones to sit on'. So a wooden chair was brought in, placed amongst the vulgar horse-hair chairs beside the mahogany table, and father sat in it never pretending that he had seen and felt the insult. The sick old miser was not worthy to tie my father's shoe-strings, and I have not repented of the inscription I placed on my father's grave-stone, applying to him what was said of 'the wisdom that is from above': 'First pure, then peaceable, gentle, and easy to be entreated, full of mercy and good fruits'; for such, in truth, my father always was. He was not in the least intellectual; he read slowly and with some difficulty and stumbled at the long words, and he read very little; he was not a social leader in any direction, nor sought to be; he was unassuming and unselfish to the last degree. His neighbours hardly knew the depth of their love and respect for him, till he was taken away; but the aroma of his character still lingers in that little village where he spent his life.

Chapter II

I believe I can claim that I learned my trade and became a sound and neat, though, so far, a slow workman. My reason for this belief is that when I was about 16 years of age the best kind of work, that which demanded the most skilful handling, was committed to me in my turn, just as to my fellow-workers. But I made no further progress, for a new ambition which changed the whole course of my life had suddenly flared across my path. The workshop and all its interests fell into the background. It hardly counted at all any more, although up to that time its power over me had been paramount and its influence, so far as I can judge, to the last degree wholesome and educative. But, while the little workshop and my working companions exercised more influence and did more to form my mind and character than anything else, there were other forces in operation. After all, the workshop was only an item in the wider and more varied life of the community, in which, perforce, I shared. For 'social influences' were at their silent and restless play. And social influences, in my opinion, are powers whose extent has never been adequately realized. They are so constant, and they are so universal, and they are so intangible. As a rule we are not even conscious of their operation, anymore than we are of the weight of the atmosphere. Their very existence is overlooked, and, for the majority of men and women, remains unsuspected.

These influences not only played around and upon the mind and character of the members of that little remote community, but, as always, they entered into them and became elements in their very structure. From their silent working came the uniqueness of the villagers of Llangernyw, making them distinguishable from the inhabitants of the neighbouring villages of Llanfair and Gwytherin. For having entered into the mind and character and become elements

Llangernyw, late 19th century. [*By permission of the National Library of Wales*]

of the personality of the villagers they shared in and coloured all their activities. In short what the food and the air and the soil and the changing seasons meant for the body, the traditions and customs of the neighbourhood meant for those who were born and brought up in it. The individual could no more escape from their power than he could escape the laws of nature, and the results they produced had something like the necessity of natural law.

Perhaps I had better try to illustrate this matter.

For many years I have professed to be a moral philosopher. As a moral philosopher I am bound, as other men are not, to analyse character, and, so far as I can, show it in the making. Above all I am committed to the thinking that is *reflective* in character, to what Carlyle would call 'unwholesome self-scrutiny'; and I am bound to put opinions and beliefs unconsciously and uncritically adopted, to rigorous tests. Does the reader believe that, in doing so, I am able to free myself of the elements introduced into my very being when I was a growing boy and youth in that quiet little village? I myself am under no such delusion. I can hardly help taking my stand at the side of the working man, or, if I think him wrong, being generous in my excuses for him. The memory of my father comes up when I try to measure the value of the services and the pay of the workers. But my sympathy for the employer and capitalist is always slow to flow; and I find myself wondering what their wages would be were they paid according to the value of their social services. Day by day I find new evidence that to be fair all round is beyond my power.

But there is another side to the picture. The social influences of my boyhood help me to avoid being the slave of my present circumstances. I can look at men and things from more than one point of view: for the constitutive elements of personality persist and renew themselves under every change. And I often feel, as I move amongst my students and my colleagues, that the little village shoemaker and Calvinistic Methodist chapel-goer has still his part in what I say and do.

Now amongst these social influences the most subtle and also the most universal were those of what goes by the name of 'religion'. A very great deal depended on whether you attended the church, or one of the two chapels. Not that there was much sectarian antagonism in those days. I never witnessed any bitterness of that kind except in the actions and sayings of the parson, of the squire's wife, and the schoolmaster. The parson could hardly be blamed. Dissent to him was simply 'sin', as bad as lying any day and far less gentlemanly and pardonable than an occasional drunken spree. Amongst the chapel-goers I can recall no evidence of antipathy to the church. When Owen Evans, the comical old joiner, said that if he saw the devil eating the parson on the high road he would not say 'Shoo' to him, it was not a sectarian but a personal quarrel. One of our elders, Robert Davies, went from the chapel service every Sunday morning straight to the church service: I did the same myself, and while a member of the Calvinistic Methodist chapel sang in the church choir. Still more significant of the good-will of church and chapel in those days was the fact that the old clerk, Robert Roberts, who led the responses every Sunday morning and afternoon in the parish church, faithfully attended our chapel in the evenings.

The one-sidedness of the squire and his wife showed itself mainly in petty favouritisms, and only later on did it play a part in the letting and refusing of farms to men wishing to be tenants. But I pass on from this petty and flavourless topic of sectarian antagonism, generally so contemptible to laymen.

What did matter was that, if you went to the same place of worship as your neighbour, other social relations of all kinds were apt to spring up between him and you. So that the summary effect was the somewhat decisive division of the villagers into two communities, whose pursuits were not always the same nor their purposes always in harmony. They voted, for instance, on different sides in politics.

The reader will permit me to dwell a little on that which I knew best — the Calvinistic chapel community.

The chapel was close by my home. Its southern gable was the boundary wall of my grandmother's little garden. Long ago there was a window in that gable, and in summer time it was usually open; and many a time did my mother listen to the sermon through that open window, as she sat in the garden with the baby in her arms and one or more of us little ones played about her knees.

I remember being myself in that garden on a Sunday evening, and passing through 'a religious experience' there which I can never forget. It was in the year 1859 or, possibly, 1860. I was about seven years old at the time, and the religious Revival was on in all its power in all the neighbouring dissenting chapels (for some reason or another the Church of England was not liable to these onsets). The evidence of the presence and power of the 'spirit' was overwhelming. Men and women were, quite genuinely, beside themselves with religious excitement. They broke out in the services, glorifying God by the help of hymns and verses, and not infrequently in language of their own which, owing to their 'exalted' condition, was sometimes marvellous in its power and beauty. Their voices mingled together in a confusion that usually put the preacher to silence, and, not seldom, lasted far into the night. Often, during those months, did I crouch in the bottom of the pew in order to escape the waving arms of my grandmother — noted for the depth and devotion of her religious life. And I, occasionally, watched strange scenes amidst the excitement. For instance, I saw a farm labourer, — a very shoddy character in fact — on his knees in the big pew, beat in the panels of the pulpit with his bare fists; and I watched the finest of the church elders, one of the ablest men I have ever met, go from end to end of the chapel and up and down its aisles, on his knees praising God all the time and mani- festly in the power of an overwhelming force.

I am not going to discuss either the causes or the spiritual value of these religious revivals, and I shall say only one thing, namely, that to doubt the sincerity of some, yea, of most of the revivalists, or the permanence of their good effects upon their lives, were dishonest and absurd on my part.

But I must return to the personal incident under the chapel window to which I have referred, for in its way it is unique.

The Revival had come to the neighbouring chapels; or, in other words, to put it quite frankly as we all thought of it, 'The Holy Spirit', the third person in the Trinity, had actually arrived at these chapels and attended the meetings. But He had not come into our chapel; and great was the searching of hearts. The prayers of the elders became more and more urgent, and the fear grew even more grave that possibly some dark sin on some one's part in our church kept the

Holy Spirit away. We were bidden examine and humble ourselves anew! and we did so. But at last the Spirit came. It was on the evening on which I was in the garden, under the chapel window. For, did I not hear, and recognise, the voices of the women, who were in an ecstatic state, mingling with the voice of the preacher, and for a while, contending with it in wild confusion? I have said that, at the time, I was about seven years old. But that did not protect my little child-soul from being suddenly overwhelmed by the conviction that I was not *one of the elect*! My reason for this conclusion was that when the Holy Spirit did come I was not in chapel. Manifestly my Calvinistic up-bringing was thorough; and even then the main joists of my creed were being laid, and by other hands than my own.

I am tempted to cite one other incident that goes to show the power of the revival. My grandmother's empty and unused pig-sty was at the side and behind her house. It was a very secret place. No one ever passed that way. In that empty pig-sty, day by day for many weeks, four or five of us schoolboys, all of them a year or two older than myself, met after the mid-day meal, and before returning to school in the afternoon held a prayer-meeting! We prayed 'for the longest', and 'for the most like' the ruling elder. While one of us prayed, the others broke in with a solemn 'H—m,' or a loud 'Amen,' or 'Glory to God,' (in imitation of our elders of course), in the deepest voice we could command. It ought not to be necessary to say that we were all in dead earnest.

That set of boys, I may remark in passing could not have been quite 'ordinary', for practically the same group acted together in other ways. We persuaded the village schoolmaster one winter to open a night school, and we attended it till some one of us detected his incompetence. Then we left him in the lurch and we met together once a week in the squire's gas-works to learn short hand. While Peter the gas-man emptied and refilled the white-heat retorts we sat baking opposite, under the single gas jet. In addition, every now and then there were competitive meetings or little Eisteddfods, whose influence by the by is admirable. So that, somehow or other there was always something 'intellectual' going on amongst us. We had our aspirations in fact, and they did not quite 'come to nothing'.

The Revival, with all its strange excellencies and absurd extrava-

Capel y Cwm, Llangernyw. [By permission of the National Library of Wales]

gances, passed off with the year 1860. Its influence remained. It marked men and women who had felt its power even although they fell away again. They were like trees that had been in a forest fire, standing — but leafless. Others lived a new life ever after, and no honest man could question either its sincerity or its excellence. Moreover the little church was 'freshened'. Its religious life owing to its experience of the Revival was more intense.

In ordinary times, as I have already hinted, the services in the little chapel were of almost daily occurrence; on Monday evening there was the weekly prayer-meeting; on Tuesday evening the children's catechising meeting; on Wednesday evening the singing meeting; on Thursday the church meeting in which our elders shared their religious experiences of the week; and on Friday evening the young men's meeting. There was no pastor: the church was too small and, at that time, the ministry of the Methodists was almost itinerant. A pair of old preachers would start at home and, preaching two or three times every day in different chapels, visited before they returned home every place of Calvinistic worship in Wales. I knew some of these old men.

As there was no pastor in our chapel the weight of 'the good cause', both spiritual and temporal, lay naturally on the shoulders of the elders. And the elders, I may say, were elected 'for life' — unless they fell away, which they hardly ever did — and they were genuine autocrats. I must not pass them without a word or two of each.

First came John Davies, who lived at one time in the thatched old cottage and afterwards in the chapel-house. He was for a while a crofter holding a little farm that kept a cow or two; but for the greater part of his life he worked as a labourer. No one ever doubted the passionate earnestness of his religion, or could forget how his public prayers shook him, body and soul. But he was passionate also in ways which were not always religious. His temper was sudden and masterful, and he often said things in anger and hurled about reproofs, for which his wife, as a rule, sorely repented.

Then there was Hugh Hughes, a little, smart, elderly slater of houses, whose wife kept a little shop and whose daughters were amongst the leaders of the village fashions. He was a very gentle soul, very modest, and, indeed, very small. I do not think he ever said anything that was not common-place, or that was worth the hearing: and the longer words in the Bible puzzled him greatly. Fortunately, however, the long words brought 'a wind upon his stomach,' and thus gave him time to spell them! Everyone respected Hugh Hughes, such was his fidelity and kindliness and honesty.

Robert Davies, the big tailor, need cause no delay. He was, in every way, ordinary. William Ellis, the farmer, was a far more living and interesting man: he was a better teacher of his adult class in the Sunday School, and he had something more fresh to say when he stood up to speak. William Ellis was one of my best friends. Many an evening, when I was a youth of about eighteen, and he a middle-aged man with children of my own age, we walked up and down the country road that led to his home, discussing the things which for both of us at that time meant most and were to be sought first.

There remains Robert Hughes, also a farmer. He suffered during all his early years from ill-health. He was an able and, in all that concerned Wales and its liberation, a highly educated and learned man. He was a most excellent teacher and, as an impromptu public speaker, without a rival in all the countryside. I owe a great deal to him. He took the Sunday School class in hand of which, with some four or five boys a little older than myself, I was a member, after all the other Sunday School teachers had refused to have anything to do with us — so endless was our mischief. He opened the Bible for the first time to me and to the other boys, and made us feel something of its qualities. The book of Job, owing to his dealing with it during my childhood, has been one of my first favourites ever after.

I cannot pretend to measure the influence of the chapel and the traditions which were current amongst those who attended it upon my life and character. I think my religious beliefs are less crude now as well as shorter than they were in those days; but the essentials of the faith, the hypothesis on which I would fain say that my life rests, and without which the world would seem to me to be a wild chaos and the life of man a tragical blunder — that remains the same. We certainly wasted none of the opportunities that the chapel offered. As a matter of fact my mother sent John and me there, where we would be safe and out of the way. We were there practically every night of the week, except Saturdays, and our Sundays were especially crowded. I wonder if the Scottish Church can beat our record. From 8.30*a.m*, to 9.30*a.m.* there was the young men's prayer-meeting which we attended after a very hasty breakfast. From 9.30*a.m.* to 10.30*a.m.* there was the public prayer meeting or a sermon. At 10.40*a.m.* I was in the parish church, singing into the ears of the rector's daughter who sat in front of me and played the harmonium. At 12 noon we had our one meat dinner of the week, ending with my mother's incomparable '*Pwdin Rice.*' At 1*p.m.* there was the young men's reading class in which we sat till the Sunday School opened at 2*p.m.* At 3.30*p.m.* the school closed; at 4*p.m.* we had tea; from 5*p.m.* to 6*p.m.* there was the singing meeting; at 6*p.m.* the chapel filled for the sermon which usually lasted till 7.30*p.m.*; from 7.30*p.m.* to 8*p.m.* there was the meeting of the church members only, mere adherents having gone home. Did ever a boy have a better chance of being either very religious, or very much the opposite? But so far as I know I was neither; for there were still other influences in operation and I shall mention two or three of them.

First, perhaps, came that of music. I was passionately fond of music, and it is one of the regrets of my life that I did not cling to it. On

Sunday afternoons, after tea, I used to go to help an old man called Nathaniel Jones to read the tunes in his hymn book. I was a very little boy, and the music was written in the standard notation. Then John Curwen popularized the sol-fa system: Eleazar Roberts of Liverpool introduced it into Wales; and, amongst those who took it up, learning it himself while teaching a class of young men, was John Price, the schoolmaster of the British School at the southern end of our parish. I would fain sing the praises of John Price, so admirably did he fill his place in the neighbourhood. But I shall have occasion to return to him.

Amongst those who attended the sol-fa class was my brother William, a joiner, a blacksmith, and a sawyer. John and I were not allowed to go: we were too young. But we broke into the private drawer of our big brother, studied his sol-fa lesson books, and learnt the system without any teacher. I was about ten years of age, and had an excellent boy's voice, and, at that time, my knowledge of sol-fa was considered something of a marvel. Later on I discovered how little there is in it — the sol-fa system for a musical child is so easy. By and by our achievement became known to Price. He gave a hint to my big brother that John and I might attend the weekly lessons; and I recall with amusement the way in which, as we walked the two miles along the road to the meeting at Pandy, John instructed me how to show my musical prowess. 'When I pass from the alto to the soprano, you, Harry, pass from the soprano to the alto! We'll make Mr. Price see that we can read.' And we did.

I think that Robert Hughes, the elder, must have been a little jealous of Mr. Price and the new system. He was the precentor in our chapel, and conducted the singing meetings in which the psalms and hymn tunes were learnt. In one of these, having broken down himself over a new hymn-tune, he taunted and challenged us sol-fa boys. John accepted the challenge on my behalf and compelled me to sing the tune, which I did all through all alone. Not long afterwards Robert Hughes ceased to precent or to be responsible for the singing in the little chapel. My brother William first, and my brother John afterwards were elected to take his place.

There is one incident more connected with this topic that may be worth describing. My father very rarely went into either of the two

village public houses. But one evening he came home from the Stag
Inn and excitedly asked for me. A farmer over his drink had denied
my ability to read at sight any tune in the church 'Tune-Book.' He
offered ten pounds against ten shillings; and my father came home to
find out from my brothers and myself whether he could take on the
bet. He received from every one of us the fullest and most confident
assurances; and, with all my soul, I begged him to go back and bet.
Then '*I would have ten pounds to buy a harmonium*'. My father did go
back, ready to take the bet. But the farmer on seeing his readiness
drew back, and, to my intense disappointment, nothing came of the
incident. My last chance of becoming a musician, if, indeed, there ever
was a chance, had gone; and, as it happened, the current of my life
took a quite other and unexpected direction.

The cause of the change looks very remote, and in a sense, really
was remote. The squire had taken to letting his larger farms to Scotch
tenants — till he learnt his lesson. At one time there was quite a
sprinkling of Scotsmen in our neighbourhood. The head gardener of
the squire was one; the chief estate agent (or factor) was another; and
there were besides, Mr. Stuart of Cammaes, Mr. Roxburgh of Cae'r
Llo, and Mr. Borthwick (afterwards a great importer of frozen meat
and a member of the House of Lords) together with their domestic
servants and shepherds and other dependents.

These peaceful but energetic invaders of the neighbourhood found
the winter evenings long and dreary. So they took a chief part in the
starting of 'Penny Readings'. The meetings were held in the village
school, were attended joyously by every section of the little
community, Welsh and Scotch, church and chapel, and were presided
over, as a rule, by the squire. The entertainment was run by the
villagers themselves, and amongst the most frequent of the
performers were my father's three boys. Indeed, it was to us that
messages of distress were sent when some singer or reciter broke
down, or when there was some gap in the programme which could
not be filled otherwise. We could read the sol-fa notation and sing in
parts, and we could also act in a little scene or recite when necessity
called. Things went very well, if I remember rightly, for at least two
winters. Then calamity came. One evening Mr. Stuart, one of the
Scottish farmers, danced a sword-dance in Highland costume on the

little stage, to the intense interest of the spectators who had never before seen anything of that kind. But, alas, the Calvinistic Methodist conscience was hurt and roused, and from that time on the 'Penny Readings' lost favour and waned to their natural death.

I can now be more directly relevant, and indicate the unexpected significance of these 'Penny Readings' performances to me. My father had taken a pair of boots that had been repaired to Mr. or Mrs. Roxburgh, or possibly to one of the servants, and was sitting, as usual after business was over, exchanging news in the kitchen, when Mrs. Roxburgh came in. 'Elias!' she says to my father (as he afterwards told me), 'I understand that that little boy with the red hair and the intelligent face who sang so well in the last 'Penny Reading' is your son. Will you send him up to me? I think he is fit for something better than shoe-making and I should like to talk to him.' My father came home, reported to my mother, as usual, and a few evenings afterwards I was sent up to see Mrs. Roxburgh. Mr. and Mrs. Alexander Roxburgh, I should say in passing, were the most respected and the best loved Scotch that ever lived in our neighbourhood. They were natives of Annan in Dumfrieshire, and had visited Llangernyw on their wedding tour and fallen in liking with the neighbourhood. Mr. Roxburgh then rented a large sheep farm from the squire, came for some years, in summer only, with his family, and lived in a remote farm-house; and then he took his permanent residence at Cae'r Llo, and made his home there. The Roxburghs were well-to-do, neighbourly, and generous almost to a fault.

Mrs. Roxburgh on being told that I had come as she desired, sought me out in the kitchen and took me at once into the parlour sitting-room. There I saw, for the first time, a floor covered by a carpet. Mrs. Roxburgh began the process of converting me without any delay, making me 'her own boy' there and then. I was, I believe, about fourteen years old at the time, and I had been for a little more than a year at the making of shoes. 'You are not made to be a shoe-maker', she said to me, 'you must give it up and go to college and become a minister'. She knew that my parents were quite poor, and that they could not pay my college fees, not to speak of maintaining me there, or paying for my board and lodgings, were it only for a single term.

But she had seen poor boys clamber into the pulpit in her own country; she had the belief in education which was characteristic of her people at that time, and she had limitless enthusiasm. The prudential considerations which have hindered so many possible enterprises were quite foreign to her nature. If she thought a thing ought to be done, she took it for granted that it could be done, and never took the trouble of considering what means should or could be employed, or what chances of succeeding there might be. Given the faith, works would follow. Let us but do our bit: Providence, always much on the alert as Mrs. Roxburgh thought, would do the rest. One thing more there was which gave edge to her aspirations for me. Her brother, George, once Provost of Annan, had studied for the ministry. At one time he was, I believe, one of the best students of Sir Wm. Hamilton's class. But his health gave way. Mrs. Roxburgh's interest in her brother's college career had evidently been very intense; she copied his lectures for him and gave every proof that his success in college was for a time her first ambition.

For some reason or another, or for none at all, Mrs. Roxburgh transferred her college ambitions from her brother, and fixed them upon me. Week by week from the first night on, I was invited up to Cae'r-Llo, and Mrs. Roxburgh spent the whole evening counselling, warning and encouraging me, and playing the piano to my singing. It mattered nothing what company she might have in the house. She persisted, and, I believe, was well teased by her more intimate Scottish friends who, every now and then, visited her in Wales. I cannot recall many details. But I remember that she warned me solemnly against reading anything written by Thomas Carlyle — of whom, by the by, I had never heard. She also lent me Pollock's *Course of Time* praising it in the strongest terms and urging me to read it. More to the purpose were successive parts of *The Popular Educator* which I borrowed from her, some of 'the home lessons' in which I learnt, in an intermittent way. But the main factor of the situation did not lie in any definite help or guidance that she gave me; but in the persistence of Mrs. Roxburgh's purpose and, still more especially, in that she never concealed her wish that I should be 'something better than a shoe-maker.' There was, she firmly held, 'no future' for me in that direction. Besides, shoe-makers as a rule were an intemperate and low set. I ought not to be one of them: I ought to become a minister.

It looked for a long time as if all her trouble with me was to go for nothing. I stood firmly by my shoe-making. I liked it, it was a thoroughly respectable trade to those who looked after themselves. Looking to the future I saw nothing out of place. I was not only to be the best shoe-maker in all the country round, but an elder in the chapel, and one of the neighbourhood's real but uncrowned leaders. Such were the convictions on which I took my stand against Mrs. Roxburgh, and I was helped no doubt by a pride of my own of which I had quite enough, and which, at that time, experience had not tamed. And so far as I can see, my pride, in that instance, was not far out of place. In any case, I continued to visit Mrs. Roxburgh week by week for some years, holding to my own views and sticking to my own purposes. But that never weakened her interest in me, or dimmed the splendour of her care for the boy of her adoption. And it was not Mrs. Roxburgh who in the end lost the contest. A time came, sudden as lightning, when my purposes went with the winds and hers held. But that is the theme of the next chapter.

Chapter III

A lad of my own age, called Tom Redfern, had come from Halkyn, near Holywell, to the village school of Llangernyw, as a pupil teacher. [He is now, and has been for many years, the much respected rector of Denbigh, and one of the canons of the cathedral of St. Asaph.] Somehow or another, in a manner which I never quite understood, Tom and I became fast friends. Our friendship was contrary to all rule and precedent: for he was 'Conscientious Church', and I was 'Conscientious Chapel'. And I think he endured some petty perse-cution on my account: for, both in religion and in social standing, I was 'beneath' him. We saw each other every day, and were together at every interval sharing our views of men and events. In short a closer or more inveterate friendship there could hardly be.

One memorable day Tom was allowed by the schoolmaster and I by my father to have a holiday. Wombwell's menagerie had come to Llanrwst, which was only seven miles away; and neither Tom nor I had ever seen a lion, or tiger, or elephant, or camel, or any of the marvels of the animal world. We went to Llanrwst early in the day, arriving long before the show opened. Then we took a walk along the streets of Llanrwst with one of my second cousins, called Sam Roberts, son of a tailor and draper in the town. Looking up the street Sam saw a group of disreputable loungers hanging around the door of a tavern. Then he turned round to me and said, 'LOOK AT YOUR SHOP-MATES, HARRY!'

He meant nothing in particular. It was a perfectly casual remark on his part. But to me it was by far the most startling event in my whole life. I was stunned and helpless. The things that Mrs. Roxburgh had told me were true! My shop-mates *were* disreputable! Their companionship in the workshop would verily be both unbearable and ruinous. Shoe-making held no future that could be respectable. Such were the thoughts that crowded in upon me. Distrust and deep repugnancy at the very thought of spending my life at shoe-making took immediate and full possession of me. The views which Mrs. Roxburgh had been pouring into my soul week by week and year by year had accumulated like dammed waters. And now the dam had broken and I was swept away as by a flood, — helpless, resourceless, hopeless. No one can pass through an experience like mine and deny either the reality or the bitterness of sudden and complete conversion. And it was permanent: for I never wavered afterwards.

But I made no reply to Sam. I got rid of him as soon as I could, and then I went, with my friend, Tom, at my side begging me to tell what had come over me, and sat on the further bank of the river Conway in an agony of weeping.

My whole life seemed to me to have been a mistake. It lay in ruins around my feet: and it was all from beginning to end my own fault. Only one thing remained. I would become 'something better than a shoe maker' or I would die in the attempt.

I suppose I must at last have given Tom some hint of my trouble. At any rate the torture slackened, I became calm, we left the river-side and entered the show. We stayed there for several hours, and somewhere about ten or eleven at night watched the animals being fed. Then, after a light supper at James Pugh's, the postman's, we started through the quiet night on our seven-mile walk home, in company for the greater part of the way with a third rural visitor to the show.

Left to ourselves, somewhere between one and two in the morning, Tom and I faced the new life-problem which had sprung upon me. It was a lovely summer night and all the world was asleep. Then when we were about a mile and a half from our village, on the bank of a little stream opposite some cottages called 'Tangraig', Tom and I shook hands over a solemn oath that, some day, we would be graduates of a university. We had London University in our minds. It did not demand attendance at lectures, or residence. We could prepare for its examinations wherever we might be and whatever our occupation. It was a rather unusual proceeding for two boys of sixteen. And we kept our oath: a year or two after I graduated in the University of Glasgow, Tom graduated at Cambridge.

But, for some time, nothing was done: Tom went on with his work as a pupil-teacher and I as a shoe-maker. There was no evidence of any outlet for me in any direction, nor a glimmer of hope. Indeed, it was not easy for me to confess my change of mind to my father and mother; I had insisted so wilfully on being a shoe-maker. But my father's sympathy was too certain and too valuable, and I was working at his side all day long, so that the confession was not much delayed. They could, however, do nothing. They were as helpless as myself.

One day, after some months of fruitless anxiety, my mother went to the other end of the parish, which was called Pandy Tudur, to attend the funeral of an old lady. After it was over it happened that Mr. Price, the schoolmaster of whom I have already spoken, asked her and her companion, a Mrs. Parry, wife of our village blacksmith, to tea, before they started on their two-mile walk home. Over the tea-cups my mother told Mr. Price of my 'uneasiness', and in her sudden way, full of insight, asked him 'Is it not possible to make him into a school-master?' Mr. Price was full of sympathy with the design, but pro-nounced it beyond the power of my parents to carry it out. 'You cannot afford it, Mrs. Jones *bach*' (dear), he said, 'You would have to keep him at his studies for at least three years before he could enter college; and it would be two years more before he would be making his own livelihood. It is too heavy a burden for you and Elias Jones. But send the boy here to me! Three months of school, at his age, will be invaluable to him whatever he is going to be; and if he is as smart over his lessons as he was over singing the sol-fa notation he should do very well.'

Such was the suggestion brought home by my mother. I was to go to school at Pandy, where there was always a bench of grown-up lads when work on the farms was slack; and I was to stay there for three months and see whether 'something would not turn up'.

It was the year 1869, and the year was at the spring, for I remember well discussing the project with my father while we planted potatoes, in accordance with a very old custom, in a neighbouring farmer's field; and discussing it *ad nauseam* had it not been my father. I did not like it. It might end in failure and in my being sent back to shoe-making, and so on. But there was no alternative, except that I was to see Mr. Price first. So, one afternoon I went, with a burden of boots on

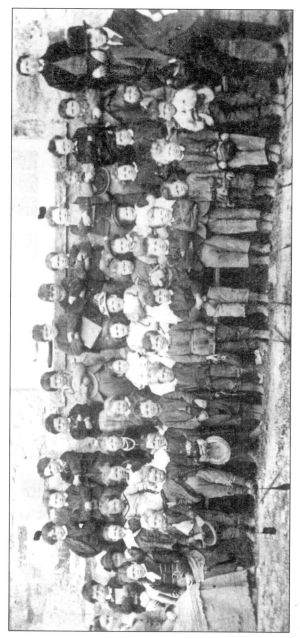

School children at Pandy Tudur School late 19th century.
The teacher on the right is probably John Price. Is the boy behind him Henry Jones?

my back both repaired and new which I had to leave at cottages and farm-houses on the way, and saw and had a good talk with Mr. Price. In the meantime he had been considering my case in his wise way; and he had formed another plan. I was to attend school for an indefinite period on three days of every week, and to pay for my keep by working at my trade on the other three days.

My joy in the new method had no bounds. I left Mr. Price's house about nine or nine thirty in the evening, ran towards home from sheer gladness of heart for a full mile, and then I turned into an old quarry by the side of the road, and opposite to the farm of Ty'n Ddol. There I poured forth my soul in gratitude to Him, who, as I believed and still believe, grants to mankind the opportunities of learning good- ness. Then I hurried to my crowded wee home, told the new plan to my father and mother, and that very night hunted out an old book of geography and began to learn the names of the counties of England. I had my chance, and I was going to seize it.

On the following Monday morning, it must have been in May or early in June, I might have been seen between eight and nine making for the Pandy School along the quiet country road. On arriving I was put at a desk, pretty well by myself, and not inserted in any children's class. There books were given me, till I could get my own; and, above all, 'sums' were set me to work out, in 'Rule of Three' and 'Weights and Measures'. I had forgotten the 'Weights and Measures', but by no means the multiplication table; and before long, I was forging ahead through Fractions, Vulgar, and Decimal, and on to Simple and Compound Interest, 'Tare and Tret' and so forth. But my progress in grammar was slower and much more laborious, I had been ill-taught in the village school, and the effects lasted, as they always do in matters of life, and character.

Meantime, on alternate days, that is, on Tuesdays, Thursdays, and Saturdays, I worked at my trade; and, by this time, I sat opposite the window instead of the workman, and side by side with my father. But every jot of enjoyment and of enterprise in the shoe-making had departed, and I used every possible occasion to slip out in order to recall some date in history, or, to solve some problem in arithmetic.

Tom Redfern, as a matter of course, knew all about the turn which my affairs had taken; and, being always the very essence of prudence and common sense, he made fun of my enthusiasm and predicted that in a week or two it would pass off. The very opposite happened.

One mid-day, with a part of his dinner in his hand, Tom ran over to see me. I gave him a hint, we left the workshop together, and crossed the style to the field at the back of the house. There I sat down and put into Tom's hands a problem in arithmetic I had been trying in vain to solve; and at the same time I had another try at it myself. As it happened the first to find the answer was myself, and the little incident had a big result. Tom was shaken out of his complacency, he caught my enthusiasm and he took up his studies in a manner he had never done before. I had, in reality, the better chance, and before long I caught him up and passed him. And he knew it for he took his lessons from me, especially in geometry and in grammar, in both of which subjects the teaching of the village school was hopelessly incompetent. Mr. Price, on his part, was in no sense a scholar. Ploughboy, as he had been, and only a few months in a London Training College, he never had a chance; and the English he spoke was very imperfect. But he had plenty of good sense and shrewdness; and, after the first few months, never meddled with me, except in the way of encouragement. It was long afterwards that he confessed how he feared to be found out by me — for, as he said 'You had no common sense! and it would never have done'.

But I must enter somewhat more fully into the details of this period of my double life, half of it in school, and half in the shoe-maker's shop.

The plan of going to school every other day was never altered. On the contrary, under every kind of pressure, my father permitted me to be faithful to it. And for a month prior to the examination for the Queen's Scholarship, my father relieved me from making shoes. Neither did I go to school. I spent the whole month 'recapitulating', in the empty and fireless chapel, where I walked to and fro all day long — 'cramming' as idlers would say, 'working' and working very hard so far as I can see. After the examination I was to repay my father with a month of unbroken shoe-making. Except during that time every Monday, Wednesday, and Friday found me in the British School, at Pandy, a good two miles from my home; and the other four days of the week found me at home.

But, in every other respect, there was a frequent change of plans. When the turmoil in our little kitchen proved insurmountable, I studied at my grandmother's next door at times. At other times I went in deepest secrecy to the cellar under Hafodunos Hall with one of my brothers, who happened to be responsible for keeping up the fire that heated the pipes which went round the house. He would leave me there, where there was a gas jet, and late at night I would make for home. It was in that cellar that I learnt the history of Henry VII, I remember, in *Ross's* text book, all in one evening.

For a while, in summer, Tom Redfern flung gravel about 4 a.m. at my bed-room window, and, much more frequently, I flung gravel at his, till his landlady interfered, and gave me a vigorous 'hearing'.

The next move was that my brother, John, and I, not without some difficulty persuaded my mother to let us sleep in the bed at the dark end of the workshop. For John was also studying, in preparation for the examination of which I have already spoken. Once installed in the workshop and work was over, John and I could do as we pleased. And our plan was for me to go to bed very early, say about 8*p.m.*, if the workshop was clear, and at 1*a.m.* John wakened me and went to bed himself. But the strain on him proved too heavy, for he worked fairly hard in the day time, and our mother struck in and put an end to the matter so far as John was concerned.

We had heard moreover, that 'one hour before midnight was worth two after midnight'. So I continued to go to bed as early as I could, say from 8*p.m.* to 9*p.m.*, and about one in the morning, before he went to bed himself, the village policeman came, every night, and tapped at the workshop window to awaken me. I got up, dressed, planted a small table before my seat, and my feet in a basket of broken pieces of leather, and sat working at my books, and working with all my might, throughout the small hours and till morning came. I wonder if the reader can guess the joy with which I heard the clatter of the breakfast tea-cups and the other sounds which showed that my mother was up.

'A hard life', you remark; and I reply 'Most certainly!' Few growing boys could have stood it; and many a time did my father try to persuade me to adopt some easier plan. But the resolve to gain a Queen's Scholarship and the right of becoming a student at the Bangor Training College for Teachers, was a madness in my blood.

Easier methods were not altogether out of reach; at one time I was tempted to adopt one of them, and in a manner that always reminds me of Bunyan's Pilgrims at By-path Meadow.

The Squire's wife, a most inveterate proselytizer, came one summer afternoon, sat on a chair outside the workshop, opposite the door, and suggested a most seductive plan. She told me that there was a preparatory class at the Carnarvon Church of England College for Teachers, expressly intended for young fellows, who, like me, wished to enter. She would contribute to my maintenance there, I rather think that she offered to maintain me there altogether. And my chances of passing would be much greater; I should have all my time for study, and I should have the guidance and the help of qualified college teachers, instead of casual lessons from the teacher of an Elementary School. What more could I desire? I would have given almost anything for such an opportunity.

But there was one obstacle. Entrance into that college meant becoming a member of the Church of England. I was not prepared for that change; and it was precisely the desire to lead me to make that change which moved her to offer to take charge of me and my destiny. It was an exact expression of her sectarian zeal, and an admirable instance of her proselytizing methods. She was offering a most tempting bribe.

I answered by raising an issue which I knew was quite secondary. I told her, and proved by quotation from the Government blue-book that Bangor College was the better college of the two; and I made no reference to what amounted to me to 'a change of religion'. She also was shy of the real issue. As to my parents, my father took no side in the matter. He simply told me to do as I liked. But somehow I felt that he approved of my resistance to the lure. My mother was more indifferent; though, I believe, with a slight leaning to the opposite side. She saw no harm in my becoming a parson provided I was a good parson. She did not realize the significance of the fact that it was a *question of principle* to me. To 'go over to the Church' would have been for me at that time 'the grand betrayal'. My character thereafter would have been broken-backed. And although the time might come, as it has come, when such sectarian differences would be to me simply contemptible, I should all the same consider that I had chosen the meaner course.

So although, like Christian, I climbed the stile, and saw a path lie along by the way, on the other side of the fence, and that there was the easiest going, I clung to my own, rougher road. The decisive refusal came a little later — there was an interview at the Hall between the Squire's wife and myself in which she lost patience and sniffed at some thing concerned with the chapel. Then I, in reply, broke out, saying that she might say anything she liked of me, but she should not scoff at the chapel and my religion in my hearing; and I struck the table and walked out of the Hall. Not long afterwards her husband sent me a present of one of his old overcoats, as a peace-making gift, I believed. But the overcoat, bless the mark! did not put out my wrath. On the contrary I had a row with my parents, because they would not let me send it back! I would fight my own battle without the help of either squire or dame.

If the reader calls these incidents petty, I shall agree with him with all my heart. But if he remembers that I would have given my life at that time to pass the examination, and that it was hard to have no help to pass except that of an elementary schoolmaster and little leisure for study except every other day, he will admit that 'the trial was sore, and the temptation sharp'. Even yet I cannot admit that 'to master it and make it crouch beneath my foot', was an insignificant matter, even though it was very small. The refusal was a very wholesome act, and I could 'go on my way rejoicing'.

The examination for the Queen's Scholarship was in December: and it was coming near. Candidates who had not been pupil teachers, had to be at least eighteen years of age, and, unless they passed in the first class, must pay an entrance fee of 10/-. These conditions being fulfilled, the student, once he had entered college, was maintained altogether by the authorities, who, in turn, received Government grants for that and other purposes.

But there was one other condition of a preliminary kind — a condition that was in practice purely formal. The candidate had to produce a certificate of character from the minister of his church. As I have said, the Calvinistic Methodist chapel in our little village had no minister: my father, therefore, naturally asked the rector, who knew me from my babyhood, to give the required certificate. He refused, exhibiting thereby the narrowest and unkindest bigotry. My father never forgave him, or attended the parish church services any more. At first the obstacle looked very serious; but a little enquiry brought out the fact that a chapel elder's certificate would serve the turn equally well; and that was easily obtained.

At last the day of the examination arrived. I had the right to compete, for I had just turned eighteen. My two brothers equipped me for the examination in the manner I have already described, and I faced the ordeal as best I could. We stayed at the college during the days of examination and became more or less acquainted with one another. I was appalled by the look of cleverness that my competitors carried and by their confidence; and I found out that while I had begun to prepare only some eighteen months before, and that under difficult circumstances, they had been preparing under much better conditions for four, five, or even six years. I did my best, but I had no jot or tittle of hope. One day, one of the college teachers, Mr. John Thomas, called me up to him when I was leaving the table at which all the candidates dined together. It was to tell me that I was doing very well, but that it was a mistake to disfigure my papers by writing above the top line and beneath the lowest line.*

I took his action to spring from sympathy with a candidate who, he knew, had no chance of entering; and his kindness altogether overpowered me. I wept like a child: I was much over-strained.

After a few days, I returned home to my father and my work, a much saddened lad; and, telling my father and mother that I had failed, I resumed the shoe-making, working all the days of the week. But I did not despair; nor dream of giving up the adventure. I was going to try again the following December. But a new idea dawned upon our minds. Could I not get an appointment as an uncertified under-master in one of the larger schools? It was worth trying, more especially because some months previously I had won certificates and also a prize from 'The Society of Arts and Science', and I could use these to support my claim. So I borrowed copies of *The Schoolmaster*,

---

* H. J. wrote above the top and below the lowest line, because (rightly or wrongly) he thought the amount of paper allowed to candidates was limited, and he had more to say than he had room for.

looked up the advertisements, and to my intense satisfaction was appointed a junior, the most junior of the masters of a school at Ormskirk, near Liverpool.

The school was private, a kind of Grammar School. It was attended by boys whose parents were in easy circumstances, or socially ambitious, and a number of them were resident. It was a new life for me, totally different from that which I had led at home; and my responsibilities were as alien as if I had been one of the Esquimaux or a Red Indian. I don't think it took the boys five minutes, after they first saw me, to give me a new name. They welcomed me as 'Copper Knob'. And I could not have been doing well, otherwise the headmaster would scarcely have roared at me from the other end of the school, when it was full of boys. But I did not lack independence; I had probably much more than I was entitled to have; so, as soon as there was a pause in the school-work, I asked to see him in his private room and I told him of a better way of behaving to me!

I believe that the headmaster was a true gentleman. At any rate, we parted with our respect for each other considerably deepened. A week or ten days later, I was at his feet a very humble suppliant, craving a favour. Two letters had been put in my hands, one from my brother and one from the college authorities at Bangor. The latter informed me that I had passed in the First Class, and at the top of the list, and was to present myself at college and begin my residence there without delay. The former was full of angry words, because I had been so impatient and had been allowed to seek and accept a post before the results of the examination were known. 'I would have tied him to the foot of the table rather than let him go', said William to my father, 'for I was sure that he would pass the examination'.

And now I had to ask the headmaster to set me free; and to his real inconvenience he did so, saying that he would not stand in the way of my future, which he believed would be very bright. Then I went and packed the little, red, wooden box which had belonged to my father and which carried my clothing. I left my waistcoat near the top. I intended pawning it in Liverpool on my way through: for I had not enough money to pay the train all the way to Abergele. However the necessity of becoming acquainted with the pawnshop never arose. In bidding me good-bye the headmaster put a ten-shilling piece into my hand, for my week's services. I regret deeply that I have forgotten his name. His kindness I shall never forget.

I arrived at Abergele with the last train, somewhere about 10*p.m.*; and, after a bite of supper at the house of one for whom I had often thinned turnips in the past, when she farmed near Llangernyw, I started on my walk of ten miles and three-quarters, along the lonely, quiet country road, meeting nobody at that hour. It was Saturday, or rather by this time, Sunday morning. I was to be in college on Monday. On the way home I was feeling at once very happy, and very unlike myself. I was, in fact, very ill: after walking some couple of miles I felt the road reeling all round me, and I kept my feet by clinging to a gate at the side. How long I was there I cannot say, nor do I remember anything else on the way home. I arrived there about four in the morning and my mother made me a cup of tea. Then I slipped into bed by John's side, and was about to get up for chapel in the morning when he called my mother and told her I was ill. She rushed upstairs at once, and sent for Nathaniel Jones, the local farrier. Either on the way to the station when I left home for Ormskirk on that memorable bright and cold winter morning, sometimes walking beside, and at other times sitting in the cart which was conveying my box to the station: or else at the school, I had caught a cold, which turned into what was then called 'inflamation of the bowels'. The country doctor was sent for; and from blotches which had broken out on my limbs and the fact that I had been away from home he diagnosed small-pox!! and treated me accordingly. But, as usual in my life, Scotland came to the rescue. Mr. Stuart of Cammaes was very ill. The local doctor was permitted to bring in a consultant — a Dr. Turner from Denbigh. Being very friendly with my father, the local doctor brought Dr. Turner to see me. He discovered at once what was the matter and changed the treatment. In about six weeks I was in the college at Bangor, so thin, and looking so ill, that, just for a little while, my fellow-students kept aloof from me for fear of some contagion.

I spent two very happy years at the Bangor Normal College. We were fed simply, but most wholesomely; the regulations as to sleep and work were most sensible, and, of course, the companionship was perfect. But when I came to look back upon much of the work we were given to do there, it was with feelings of deep resentment. The tutor from whom we learnt our mathematics, Mr. John Thomas, we found in every way admirable. He was patient, methodical, honest, and thorough. After the training I had received at his hands, the mathematical work I had to do in order to pass into the university and win its degree was comparatively easy. But it was otherwise with our study of English, and of history, etc. In these departments, methods of shameless 'cram' had been adopted; and it was not till I was in Professor Nichol's class, in the University of Glasgow, that I had even a glimpse or bare conception of what one of the greatest of our national treasures meant, namely, our literature. We analysed, parsed, and paraphrased every passage in *Julius Cæsar*, the play pre-scribed, and we could repeat most of it by heart; but we were never induced nor encouraged to read any other of Shakespeare's plays, nor to acquaint ourselves with any one of the great classical writers. Thomas Carlyle was a discovery of my own: I happened, while standing on the ladder in the library, to open *Sartor* where Teufelsdrokh, sitting in his tower, describes the seething city-life beneath him. I sat on the ladder, reading on and on. It was a case of love at first sight, and my young admiration has but deepened with the years.

The Principal gave us a Bible lesson once a week; otherwise, so far as I can remember, we did not see him. It was Mr. Thomas who did his best for the students of that college and gained their lasting trust and affection.

During the two years I spent at Bangor College, my eldest brother was gardener at Bodlondeb, near Menai Bridge, in the service of a wealthy and unique old bachelor, called Robert Davies. My brother lodged with the old man who looked after the Suspension Bridge, in a cottage built at its Anglesey end. I used to visit him on our half-holidays, on Wednesday and Saturday afternoons, taking with me one or more of my college friends. We thought the tea at which we sat with him superb; and a more warm-hearted welcome than that which went with it was not possible. At one time several weeks elapsed without my going to see him; and he scolded me well. I did not confess to him that I hadn't a penny to pay the toll for crossing the bridge. At another time I remember receiving a present from my father; and I confess that, even yet, I take a kind of pathetic pride in it. It consisted of five penny stamps.* Certainly, I was poor! but I never felt the poverty pinch, and a more free and independent soul there could hardly be. I had no money about me; but I needed none. The college fed me far better than I was fed elsewhere; and I was quite decently clad. The village tailor had, most willingly, undertaken to supply me with all the clothes I would require, and I was to pay him with the first money I earned as a schoolmaster.

So far as I can remember there were no exciting incidents during my two years at Bangor. We attended concerts occasionally, and sang in chorus under the leadership of Mr. Thomas. At his bidding also I sang bass solos on more than one occasion; and also recited, once at Menai Bridge carrying the audience with me in imagination over the Niagara Falls. It was all a very innocent and simple-minded life. And I had what was to me a matter of deep satisfaction at the time, the pleasure and honour of keeping my place throughout at the top of the college list.

But I never deemed myself in any sense a favourite of any of my teachers. One reason was that in every instance of a college row I was in arms against the authorities; and another was that I was proud and fiery to an absurd degree. 'You will do well as a schoolmaster', said my best friend, Mr. Thomas, to me, 'provided you don't quarrel with your committee'. My resignation, as I shall relate hereafter, was in the hands of the committee in about a week after I had entered its service!

I must, however, return to the college. On the evening of the last day of our last year, it was the habit of the Principal to call the students one by one to his private room; and there, in the presence of Mr. Price or Mr. Thomas, he assigned a school to them. We could either accept or refuse; but I think we invariably accepted. He had already virtually decided matters by correspondence with the local school committees. At last I was called in to find Mr. Thomas with the Principal; and the Principal told me that he regretted that for the present he could offer me no school. My disappointment was deep, but, as a matter of course, turned into angry resentment on the spot. 'It is what I

---

* His father got a sixpence for some odd job, and there were only *five* penny stamps because the sixth was used on the envelope.

expected', I said, 'and I don't care. I shall go on with my trade'.* 'What is your trade?' asked the Principal. 'Shoe-making, sir', I said, 'and I am not ashamed of my trade'. I could see Mr. Thomas sitting back and shaking with laughter. He knew that the Principal had once been a tailor and that the memory brought him anything but pleasure.

On the morrow I went home. The day after I had my leather apron on, and I was extraordinarily proud of my humility as I worked at my father's side: 'The brightest scholar in college condescending to make shoes!' was that not a spectacle for men and angels?

This folly lasted for some few weeks, when the Principal invited me to see him. I found on arrival that, in accordance with the resolution of the committee of the college, he could offer me a temporary tutorship at the college pending the coming of a new and permanent tutor.

It was in the mind of the college authorities, and of the Principal himself to propose this at the time of my interview with him, and I was much ashamed of myself. I was to share the Principal's sitting-room, a cup-board in which was emptied in order to make room for my books. I was ashamed to find that the whole of them would not fill one shelf, such had been my *literary* training! I had not, in fact, 'learnt to read' in any full meaning of that phrase.

The responsibilities of my new office were not light, and my task was not easy. Amongst other things, on most days of the week, it was my business to secure and preserve order during the evening hours of private study, and even to see the students into their dormitories. There were some sixty of them, mostly about my own age, and a half of them, now second-year students, had been fellow-students of mine the year before.

---

*The better Normal students naturally got the better schools. They were often awarded more or less in order of merit by the college authorities. Henry Jones had passed out of the Normal College at the head of the list, and considered he had a fair claim to a school. He thought at the time that he had been 'passed over', for a school, because of his share in student rows with the powers that be. Hence the resentment.

Things might have gone wrong, but somehow they did not. The second-year students formally resolved to support my authority in every possible way; and started that unbroken course of gentlemanly and respectful behaviour which I have experienced from students for nearly fifty years.

I cannot now remember what, in addition to music, I was responsible for teaching; and, except for the fact that the three or four months passed most happily and for my close intimacy and love for Mr. Thomas, that period of my life is now as a dream.

The tutor was about to arrive. The committee of a school connected with the iron and tin works and probably with the coal mines at Brynamman, the workers in which all paid a poundage towards the school's support, were advertising for a master. I applied and I was appointed.

Chapter IV

It was in the early part of the year 1873 that I took charge of the Elementary School at Brynamman. I was then twenty years of age.

Brynamman is a mining village on the borders of Carmarthenshire and Glamorganshire; and fifty years ago, in addition to coal-mining, the smelting of iron and the making of tin were carried on. It was my first acquaintance with miners and puddlers and iron and tin-workers.

The school was new: the boundary walls had not been built. It consisted of one long room with several large windows and a separate porch and lobby for the boys and the girls, together with a class-room opening out of it; and there were about 190 children's names on the school register. It is almost a matter of course that a man's successor as a schoolmaster hears that the school has been neglected. In this instance I believe the charge was to a great extent true. The number of children on the school books should have been considerably larger, judging by the size and number of the families in the neighbourhood. Their attendance was very irregular, and there was an atmosphere of leisure and boredom about the school, which is not a good sign. No lessons at all were given to, or required of, the four 'pupil-teachers' of whose education the headmaster had special charge; and the natural consequence was their neglect of their studies and weak official reports.

These circumstances were obviously my opportunities; and in some respects I was well equipped for making the best use of them. I was full of enthusiasm, both for education in general and for my own office. The proof of this was convincing; for on my way to Brynamman to take charge of the school, both of my elder brothers met me at Chester; and, as we all three sat on a bench in the public park there, I persuaded them both to give up their situations as head-gardeners and follow me to Brynamman in order to recommence their studies. For some time the three of us lodged together at the house of the minister of the Independent chapel. But after some months, William found the elementary studies irksome; he returned to his calling and became the head-gardener of the Godsalls of Iscoed Hall, near Whitchurch, Shropshire. John stayed with me much longer.

Besides enthusiasm I had health, and abundant energy. I doubt if there was a boy in the whole school who enjoyed the mid-day games more than I did; and on many an afternoon the interval for games was unconsciously prolonged and the children were in the playground with me, when we ought to have been at our lessons in the school.

I was exceedingly happy while at Brynamman. For some reason or another the neighbourhood was at my back, from the first: I *felt* the goodwill of my neighbours, and their readiness to approve anything I did — if it was at all possible. Moreover, the school flourished amazingly. In a few months the names on the school-register had gone up from some 190 to over 430. The long room and class-room were over-crowded; there was no room for the children on its floor; I had classes in the open-air, in the play-ground, when the weather was fine. When it was wet, I crowded classes into the lobbies, where the boys hung their caps, and the girls their hats and cloaks, and crammed the children amongst the wet clothing in the bad atmosphere. Although the school was new, an addition had forthwith to be built to it, as large as the original building.

In all my work I was loyally supported by the young lads I had as 'pupil-teachers 'and by my brother, John. He had been appointed 'Assistant Master,' though uncertified; and he was known, by young and old as, 'John, *brawd Mishtir*' — the South Wales version of 'John, Master's brother' — a rather humiliating title for an elder brother. He was undoubtedly 'a born teacher'. The children were extravagantly fond of him. They were soft wax in his hands; but I must also add that he was apt to be soft wax in theirs. And his methods were unique. The progress of the class which happened to be in his care was always amazing: but so was the noise it made. For that reason it was arranged that the class in his care should meet, not in the big room, but in the class-room by itself. But even that precaution was not adequate at all times. I remember going to him there one day and expostulating with him on account of the row. 'Leave me alone', he

The three brothers: William, Henry and John.

replied, 'they are learning like anything'. 'Well!' I answered, 'no one else can learn! What in the world are you doing with them?' He explained. He had hit on a new and most admirable plan. 'You see', said he, 'I have told the boys that those who are long over their sums, and whose sums are wrong in the end, are just donkeys. Now, donkeys are made to carry. Very well! the three boys at the top of the class, whose sums are right and first finished, are allowed to ride three times round the class on the backs of the three boys at the bottom of the class.' This, I thought, was to outrun all limits, and John, most reluctantly, gave up his novel method of eliciting hard work.

Personally, I do not think that I showed any originality, except, perhaps, in the way of school punishment. I had seen enough as a child of the miscellaneous and continual use of the cane. I thought 'corporal punishment' should be rare, and the master's last resource. Moreover, I think it was in the *Life of Arnold of Rugby* that I had learnt that the punishment ought to fit the crime, and, if possible, make it ridiculous.

An example or two will make my method clear. Soon after I went there as headmaster I caught a boy making faces at me — behind my back. The class, of which he was a member, sat at the time in the desks; so I invited him to come out in front and make faces in a way that let every one see him. He was very unwilling: and I had to be imperious and put on compelling threats. I told him that I was going round the school, and if he did not make faces for the class to see him, before I came back, I should punish him. This process had to be repeated. The lad found it difficult to make faces to order, and I was very loath to give up my plan. But, at last, a roar of laughter from the class told me that the boy had obeyed. I found him blubbering and sent him to his place; and, so far as I know, the custom of making faces died on the spot. There was no longer any merit or fun in it.

Let me give you another example. There were two boys in the upper class who seemed to me to be constitutionally and incorrigibly lazy. They would loll at their desks, and lie their whole length on the bench when they got an opportunity, and I frequently reproved and warned them. But I could think of no good method of dealing with their habit, far less of breaking it. However, there was a long table in the big room; and one warm summer afternoon, when being lazy was almost pardonable, having caught the boys lounging, I spread some girls' cloaks on the table and made a comfortable bed on it, and ordered the boys to take off their boots, and climb up and lie down, while I 'lapped' them round in the most motherly fashion I could command. I intended to make the boys ridiculous. But it seemed for a time as if my plan was going to fail; for the boys were big, and they looked like being shrewd enough to take it all in fun. However, to do so, proved to be beyond their power. One of them began to cry, and before long the other joined him. Then I pretended that I thought they were not comfortable, and brought more clothes; but I had to relent, and let off the two lads sadly humbled. Ever after that a reminding look was enough of a spur to either of them.

Experience of some parts of the Highlands has taught me what tidy and cleanly homes Welsh wives and mothers secure for their husbands and children. This was true even of the mining village of Brynamman. Miners' and puddlers' and iron-smelters' children, as those who came under my charge all were, they were kept very neat and clean. Nevertheless, in summer, when the roads and the play-ground were dusty and the children grew hot over their games, they were apt to come to school, especially in the afternoons, with hands and faces which were not clean. I warned the school repeatedly, without any discernible result; and at the same time I tried to think of a way of dealing with the matter. So one especially hot day, I let the children play rather longer than usual at mid-day, called them hurriedly into the school, and, for the first lesson, went on as usual. At the end of the first lesson, every slate and book was put aside, and the children were told to sit still. Then I called up into the middle of the room some eight or nine boys whose faces, as I had ascertained, were picturesque with dirt, and who, I thought, would stand the ordeal in a good-humoured way. Then I sent out for water in the school buckets, and also for soap and clean dusters. When all was ready I stripped off my coat, turned up my sleeves, rubbed the faces of the boys well with a long bar of soap, handed the boys over to the pupil teachers to dry, and sent them back to their places. If a boy showed signs of breaking down, I spared him at once. But most of the group joined heartily in the fun of the school, which was uproarious; for, of course, 'order' had gone with the winds. But a word restored it. The children returned to their places and the school resumed its work. That night the tale of the washing was told in every home, and it was enjoyed. The parents flung their influence on my side and for months afterwards, when the bell rang for the resumption of school in the afternoon, both sides of the stream that flowed near by, could be seen lined with school children washing their hands and faces. The School Inspector could hardly have approved my methods: but he did not know about them. And I recognise quite clearly that they might not have suited another teacher, or even another locality. Nevertheless, I cannot pretend to repent. They were so effective and so good-naturedly backed by the parents.

But undoubtedly that which helped most to win for me the support of the homes, and the perfect discipline of goodwill of the children in the school, was the school music. For everything was not altogether easy at first. I have already mentioned the slackness in the school: I could have added that the interest of the parents in it was very low. But at times they made it exceedingly lively. It was a custom, mainly amongst mothers, to come to the school every now and then, during the school hours, and in the presence of the children, to tell the master what they thought of him. The language was apt to be as strong as the temper was high, nor (if I was told the truth) did the women always keep their hands off the master — for there were rough specimens amongst them, more vigorous and direct than restrained in their methods.

I had to deal with this difficulty, but only once. About a week or ten days after I took charge of the school, a broad-chested and bare-armed lady came, to relieve herself of some of her less controllable convictions. I was not able to follow what she said in all its detail, for I was not as yet acquainted with the South Wales dialect; but I recognized that her wrath had been kindled by one of the pupil-teachers. I stood and listened and waited without saying one word till she stopped. Then I asked the names of all her children, and called them to my desk, in the middle of the room, from the different parts of the school where their classes sat. There were four or five of them. When they were all gathered together around their mother I asked her to leave the room, take the children with her and not send them back until she received special permission. She was rather disconcerted by the novel method of the new teacher, and she seemed somewhat disappointed as she left the school with her little troop. My next step was to write a letter to the secretary of the school, and place my resignation in his hands, if the School Committee did not approve and support my action. This is the incident to which I have alluded already in a previous chapter. I was supported much more strongly than I desired. The Committee not only permitted me to refuse applications for the re-admission of the children, but turned the father out of the works for many weeks!

The method proved effective. I experienced only one incident of a similar kind afterwards, and it had a very comical aspect. I had kept a little boy '*in*' at mid-day, for some slight mis-demeanour. He was wanted by his mother to carry his father's mid-day meal: so she came for him. I happened to be at my desk. She called her boy and he started coming. I just said 'Tom!' to him, in a severe voice, and he went back. If he was not between the devil and the deep sea, he was in a situation that was analogous; and his helplessness was so comical that I relented and 'Hannah Blaen Pal' triumphed. She was a well-known character amongst the miners' wives.

So was Tom! For, unless my memory deceives me, Tom was the only child of the four hundred and more under my care who had no ear for music. For the natural endowment of both parents and children was, in that respect, amazing. In the circumstances, my own fondness for music was a real piece of good fortune; and I indulged it to the full. Every few days I introduced a new school song. We 'practised' it as a rule at the end of the first lesson in the morning, as the children changed places from the open floor to the desks and from the desks to the open floor. To hear the song a couple of times was quite enough for the majority — enough for the tune, but not for the words. We all alike cared far too little for the words.

I do not believe that an advanced musician of the modern type would approve my method. There was little procedure 'according to rule' either in 'voice discipline' or aught else. It was not necessary, I thought, to make plans for training black-birds and thrushes; and song was not more natural to the birds than to my children. They sang with fervour and enthusiasm and passion, watching keenly the series and signs I had invented, and in which I emphatically indulged as I stood on a chair in the middle of the long room. If it was not beyond their power to go wrong, as I once heard Dr. Caird say of real genius, it was certainly far easier for them to go right.

We had two school concerts while I was headmaster. They were held in the Independent chapel, which was the largest building in the village. The floor of it was occupied by the children, for I made no selection. Every boy and girl in the school even Tom — belonged to the choir. The parents and big brothers and sisters sat in the galleries — a most enthusiastic audience, I need hardly say. In one of the two concerts the children performed the *Cantata of the Birds*, by Dr. Joseph Parry. The *Eagle* was sung by myself for it demanded a bass voice; but the *Wren*, immediately after, was sung by a group of some seven or eight little boys and girls, none of them more than six years old; and Tom took my place and led them, making signs for *piano, forte* and so on, in comical imitation of my own ways. It was both funny and charming.

In the other concert, miscellaneous songs were sung, and amongst them Handel's *Hallelujah Chorus*. There rarely, if ever, was a more mad enterprise than that of teaching a whole school of children, boys, girls, and infants, the *Hallelujah Chorus*; even although the miners took, of their own accord, to giving their help with the tenor and bass. The miners who had been working in night, or early morning shifts, used quietly to shove open the school-room door about 3.30 in the afternoon, and group themselves standing around the door, and by and by, without a word from me, they would strike in.

During the war, after an absence from Brynamman of more than forty years I visited the place. The warmth of the welcome I received from men and women, now grandfathers and grandmothers, — for miners marry very young — who had been children with me in school, touched me deeply; and the chairman, an old friend called D. W. Lewis, who was a professional musician, told the audience of an incident of the days long past which I had quite forgotten. The reader may remember that in the *Hallelujah Chorus* there are long sustained notes. According to Mr. Lewis I found the little children's breath too short to hold out; so I divided them into two parties of whom the second was to come in gradually as the first was becoming exhausted. It is almost the only original contribution to music of which I can boast.

I had happy charge of the school for about two years and when I left Brynamman evidence, of a kind which in some ways was unique, was given to me of the goodwill of the neighbourhood. Someone mentioned in one of the public-houses on a Saturday evening that I was leaving for college on the following Monday morning. During that interval, without a committee or organization of any kind, a testimonial of over £27 was collected for me: and there were friends at the train, who had not had an opportunity of contributing, begging my acceptance of their half-crowns! I lift off my hat in reverence and gratitude when I think of the working men and the working women of Brynamman.

But I must go back a little in my narrative. One evening, when I was still happy in my work as schoolmaster, I walked to the church-meeting of the Calvinistic Methodists with an old stone-mason, called Daniel Evans. We were very close friends and I ventured to tell him under what I took to be a promise of strict secrecy, that someday I intended giving up school teaching and becoming a minister. I finished my confession just as we entered the chapel. The opening service of praise, reading the Bible and prayer, was conducted as usual, and then Daniel Evans stood up in the big pew, and, to my astonishment, informed the church of the intention of which I had just told him. I was thoroughly puzzled as to what I ought to do. But a passage from Shakespeare's *Julius Cæsar* rose in my mind, 'There is a tide in the affairs of men, etc.' I resolved to let matters take their way. So word was sent from the church to the next meeting of the Presbytery, informing it that there was a young man who had expressed a desire to begin to preach, and requesting it to send a messenger to interview the young man in the presence of the church and take the voice of its members.

The choice of the Presbytery fell upon the Revd. Thomas James of Llanelly. He had once been a puddler, but had worked his way into the University of Glasgow and taken its degree of M.A. A believer in the intermittent interest of the divine being in human affairs would take this incident as an example of the intervention of a 'Special Providence': those who believe that the interest is constant can omit the word 'special'. What signifies is that the choice of Mr. James was a most fortunate one for me. An answer I gave to his question, asked in presence of the church, — 'What is your motive in wishing to be a preacher?' — seemed greatly to please him. My reply was that I did not know. 'Sometimes, I think it just a desire for any kind of public attention, or notoriety; at other times I think it is a desire to do some good.' I could give no guarantee. He called the reply unusually frank and honest, took an interest in my well-being from that moment and, above all, told me of a Dr. Williams's Scholarship for which, after a time, I might compete and which, if I won it, would maintain me at the University of Glasgow. The scholarship, I may say, is open for competition about once a year to young men, living in England and Wales, intending to enter the nonconformist ministry of any Protestant church; and its value used to be £40 a year for three years. The competition was held in London.

It was the custom among the Calvinistic Methodists in those days for pulpit aspirants to begin preaching at once; so that, almost from the time of Mr. James's visit, I wreaked my eloquence on such churches as invited me. And they were by no means slow to do so — least of all the small churches; for it was the promises made to the small churches which were most apt to be broken, so as to leave the pulpit vacant, but for the young aspirants. I was naturally asked soon, and frequently, to preach in my own church, at Brynamman; and on one occasion I invented and went through an ordeal, which I did not find it necessary to repeat. Having found that in preaching I was relying on my manuscript and taking to reading my sermon — a fatal defect in those times — I resolved to break myself of the habit. So, in the first place, I wrote out my sermon in a large book which it was impossible for me to conceal. Then I put the book down at my foot in the pulpit. Next, I began my sermon, and in a few minutes 'stuck dead'. Then I stooped down for my MS, held it up, looked for the place whence I could start again, and put the book down again at my foot. To the amused sympathy of the audience this process was repeated several times; and my best friend, Daniel James, a miner, called me a fool, for spoiling a good sermon by my nonsense. One trial of this piece of self-imposed discipline secured the desired end. I was never afterwards a 'reader' of my sermons: but I could preach with merciless eloquence from the shortest notes, or even from none at all. And I preached practically every Sunday in some one of the smaller churches of Carmarthenshire and Glamorganshire; and, in particular, I was a kind of curate, or makeshift, for the Revd. William Prydderch, who was a very popular preacher and apt to promise more than he could perform.

One natural, if not inevitable, result of this practice was that when I returned to Brynamman, at the earliest possible moment on Mondays, I was hardly fresh enough to face my work as headmaster. I lost interest in it, it began to bore me; and I began to spill any merits I had as a master at a very fast rate. So, as soon as my second school inspection was over and the certificate was gained which relieved me of my obligations to the Normal College, I resigned the school. It was, I think, the month of May, 1875. My brother, John, had departed some time before. He got married, and accepted a place as head-gardener, near Market Drayton.

I now devoted myself exclusively to my studies; and these studies were directed exclusively towards the examination for a Dr. Williams's Scholarship, which was to be held in the following October, and for which I intended to compete. At first I enquired for some Grammar School, or Grammar School teacher who could take charge of an 'adult,' such as I was, and give me special help for my examination. All my enquiries were fruitless. However, the new minister of my own church, a Revd. Thomas Lloyd, had been for a session or so in the University of Glasgow: so I went and stayed in the farm-house where he also lodged and became his pupil. But the pupillage was most unreal. For a little time at first he listened to me repeating my Latin and Greek 'Declensions and Conjugations' — which by the way he had himself forgotten — then, later on, when I began to read Greek, he helped me to find parts of the verb in the dictionary; but his help finally dwindled into keeping the English translation of the Greek or Latin author in his hands while he listened to my rendering of it aloud.

Once more, the passion for hard work and the feeling of a 'neck-or-nothing' enterprise possessed me. I was at my books at six every morning, and, except during meals and, at most, for some half hour in the afternoon, I was still at my books at midnight. The sequence of my studies was carefully considered, from the point of view of engaging 'different mental powers,' or more simply and correctly, of varying the mental processes. After an hour of learning Greek or Latin grammar, I had an hour of algebra or geometry: and I learnt the history of Greece, and the history of Rome from text-books which I read in the open-air. For there was a moor behind the house, and I walked daily there for two hours in the morning, if the weather permitted, and I committed my histories to memory by repeating the accounts of the facts in a loud voice, so as to have the help of the ear.

During these five months of very hard study I took one half-holiday; and I preached practically every Sunday. The mathematics I had learnt at Bangor, under Mr. John Thomas, was almost sufficiently advanced and I was fond of it; but in my classical studies I had to begin with the first elements. The few scraps of Latin grammar I had learnt had been forgotten, and I had to learn the Greek alphabet anew. Nevertheless, during those five months I read, and read some three times over on an average, the first book of the Iliad, the eighth book of Herodotus, a book of the Georgics and of the Æneid, Sallust's Jugurthine War, a book of Livy, and a book of the Odes of Horace. I also tried to learn to write Latin Prose, and worked right through a text-book on that subject. But I had little guidance of any other kind: for Mr. Lloyd was helpless.

Equipped with that most limited and hurriedly-acquired amount of classical learning, I went up to the Dr. Williams's Library in London, and sat the examination. There was one other competitor only, a Mr. Dryburgh, who had competed for the scholarship the year before and already spent a session at the University of Glasgow. The result was announced in a very few days. Mr. Dryburgh had done better than I had in classics and gained a few more marks; but I had more than made up on the mathematical papers, and stood first. The trustees awarded a scholarship to each of us; they were so well satisfied with the competition and the difference between us was so small.

There was, however, one condition more which I had to fulfil: unless I passed the Preliminary Examination in Glasgow, so as to enter the senior classes in the Classics at once, I retained the scholarship for one year only. I had therefore to face another examination on arriving in Glasgow. I just managed to pass, partly no doubt because one piece of 'the unseen' Greek happened to be taken from the first book of the Iliad, the only Greek book, save one, which I had ever read!

My course as an undergraduate thus began with the month of November, 1875, just before I reached my twenty-third birthday.

Chapter V

The preliminary examination of which I spoke in the last chapter, the passing of which entitled me to become a member of the graduating classes in Greek and Latin, thoroughly exposed my lack of training and ignorance of the ancient classics. I could make but little, for instance, of the passage from Xenophon's *Anabasis* given in the Greek paper, and translation from English into Greek was altogether beyond the limits of my attainments. The Professor of Latin held a test examination soon after the class was formed. The results placed me in the Fourth Class, next to the few students regarded as hopeless. I was thus distinguished in two ways from the majority of my fellow students. I was some five years older than the great majority of them, and my scholarship was poorer both in quality and quantity. There were a few students, however, who excelled me in both these respects: they were both older and more ignorant. These came, for the most part, from the Western Highlands, and were invariably making for the ministry, — of the Free Church as a rule. There being no compulsory entrance examination, they could become members of the college classes simply by paying their fees; and while occasionally a very bright and able student appeared amongst them, the great majority of them were hardly capable of being benefitted by the training which the university could offer. As a matter of fact, their becoming university students at all was regarded by them as an irksome secular interference, diverting them from and postponing their more sacred duties; for they were out to save souls. Hence, so far from seeking to widen their outlook and liberate their minds by their training, they kept their souls from first to last, securely locked, barred and bolted against all the influences of the university. Occasionally they were sources of great fun for their fellows — their renderings were so original and their answers to their professors were so unexpected. The fun was uproarious when Professor Ramsay, in his most hectoring manner, told a Highland student who had not brought his Latin exercise that he *must not let that occur again*. Professor Ramsay had failed, while the students had succeeded, in catching the excuse offered by the culprit. It was that his wife had presented him with a little daughter during the night!

If I happen not to mention the names of some of the professors of the University of Glasgow at that time, the reader will understand that their influence upon me was some what evanescent. The Greek professor was Sir Richard Jebb, a pre-eminent scholar and a most vigorous teacher. It was his first session, and, probably in consequence of having been told that some of the classes were not always quiet, his discipline was, at that time, excessively minute and strict. But the class by no means failed to realize the beauty of his rendering of the *Antigone* in the afternoons, or to be inspired as well as guided by his scholarly example. He grew in favour with his students from year to year, and had he not been succeeded by Gilbert Murray the loss to the university would have been most grave.

During this my first session I crept up in the Latin class from the neighbourhood of the dunces at the bottom, to that of the brighter spirits near the top. But Denney,* the best scholar of that year, seemed to belong to another sphere than the merely terrestrial one on which we dwelt. His scholarship was so ripe and full. In the Greek class I was awarded the eighth and last prize, which I quite deserved. But there were two or three other students who deserved it quite as much as I did. Immediately after the close of the classes the examinations for degrees were held. They were three in number — the classical, the mathematical and physical, and the philosophical and literary. The books prescribed for the examination in classics were, for the most part, different from those which we had read in the classes; and they were read and studied privately, side by side with the class work, by those students who thought they would not be in the running for class honours. Not being one of these I sat the degree examination, and had the pleasure of seeing my name honoured with a cross by the examiner, Professor William Wallace, of Oxford. My papers seem to

---

* Afterwards Principal Denney, United Free Church College, Glasgow.

have been very satisfactory. My first contact with philosophy was an incident of the Latin *viva voce*; for, with a few questions upon the meaning of a passage in one of the prescribed books, Professor Wallace had at once profoundly interested and helplessly entangled me. I never forgot my first meeting with that unpretentious great man.

During this, my first session, which had thus ended happily, I had taken the graduating class in pure mathematics, paying very little attention to its demands, which were by no means heavy. I needed all my time for the study of Greek and Latin; and I now worked less passionately hard. Circumstances would not have permitted it; for I shared a small back-room with another Williams's scholar, called William Bell. Small as it was, it was both our bed-room and study. We paid 4s. a week each for the room and attendance, and were cared for delightfully by Mrs. and Miss Work. Our weekly bill moved up and down between 10s. and 12s. a week. It was, even in those days, a small expenditure; but, so far as I can remember, Mr. Bell and I were like the disciples in the one thing that we 'lacked nothing'.

I have little to say about the summer vacation, except for a short period at Bala College, reading Plato's *Republic* with Principal Lewis Edwards and idling. I lived at home with my father and mother who, by this time, had moved from the old home at Cwm into the village. I preached every Sunday, and was received everywhere with excessive kindness. Indeed, I was offered the pastorate of more than one church during that and the following summer; but fortunately I had the sense to go on with my course at the university.

During my second session at College, namely 1876–77, I took the classes of moral and natural philosophy; and in doing so broke a regulation, of which I was ignorant, which prescribed that these classes should be taken after logic and English literature. My reason for taking my classes in an unusual order was that, by my method, I could sit my degree examination in mathematics and physics at the end of the second session, and thus avoid the necessity of sitting both in these subjects and in the philosophical subjects the same year. I exaggerated greatly the difficulty of attaining the degree standard.

The graduating class in natural philosophy was nominally conducted by Lord Kelvin; but he appeared less often than his assistant, Mr. Bottomley. It met every week-day except Saturday at 9 a.m., and our experience as students was decisively unique. When Kelvin was with us, we were being taught by the greatest physicist, and one of the worst teachers of his time. No one could predict his theme, nor his method of treating it. His lecture might be too far advanced for the best student in the class, or it might be the opposite. And Kelvin was so full of his subject as to find infinite suggestion in practically any object that caught his eye. I remember for instance that he lectured for a whole hour on 'breaking glass' — he had seen a broken window on his way to the class-room; and, as a matter of course, his exposition of his subject led him to bring in the whole solar system. Lord Kelvin's greatness as an investigator and inventor put his time deeply in his debt.

His fellow-professor Edward Caird put his time in his debt through his students. He made bankrupts of them in the first place, so great was his power as a teacher, so hard did he toil for his classes, and so impressive and beautiful was his character. I have had the rare good fortune of sitting at the feet of more than one great teacher, amongst them, Robert Hughes, the elder of the little church in Llangernyw, Sir Richard Jebb, and John Nichol. But not even these could I rank with Caird, from any point of view. He was a very learned man in his subject; and the openness of his mind, the breadth of his outlook, the sincerity and depth of his convictions, the impressiveness of his personality, made him, I believe, one of the greatest teachers of philosophy in modern times. His treatment of his subject was historical, but one never dreamt that he was dealing with dead systems of doctrine. We felt, rather, that we were being introduced into the presence of a world-old dialectic which never ceased. Under his guidance we could watch the refining of the world's experience from age to age, and observe its slow garnering and conquest of spiritual truth. To be in his class was to me, as, indeed, it was to most students, an entirely new experience. The notion of 'order,' or 'discipline' never occurred to any of us: they were things below the horizon, and any breach of them was beyond the bounds of possibility. We took notes of his lectures with all the speed we could command; and we treasured them. Notes of the lectures of one or two other professors could be borrowed or bought, for they varied hardly at all from year to year. One of the professors is said to have rebuked a student for not taking notes, and to have received the excited and unwelcome answer: 'Please, sir, I have got my father's.' The story may not be true but it deserves to be.

On one occasion only, so far as I ever heard, did a spirit of levity invade the moral philosophy class. It was when Caird lectured — and that for a full hour — on the relations of 'Bowl and Sody,' when he meant 'Soul and Body.' During that lecture he was seen, every now and then, to lift his well-known single eye-glass to his eye, and peer at the class in a puzzled fashion.

I have taught university students, as Professor of Philosophy, for more than thirty-five years, and I have had the like good fortune: there has never been any need of even thinking about order or discipline. But I doubt if any class I have ever taught could have stood the strain for a full hour of listening to me lecturing about the 'bowl' and the 'sody.'

Edward Caird's power over his class was even more fully expressed in the depth and permanence of his influence, especially in the case of the best students. Old things passed away, never to return. There was never any direct negative criticism of the traditional beliefs which we had, like others, accepted without examination or criticism. We were led, rather, to assume a new attitude of mind; and articles of our creed simply became obsolete. When I entered the moral philosophy class, the story of Jonah gave me no difficulty: and had Jonah been credited with swallowing the whale, I should have had no difficulty. And as to denying the story as it is told, on the biological ground that the throat of the whale is small and that he lives on small sea-creatures, I would have agreed with the reply of the Welsh preacher, who tossed the anatomical argument on one side with contempt, and said 'My brethren! if the Lord wanted a whale with a big throat, he could have made a whale into which the Great Eastern could pass at one end and come out at the other end without striking a single sail.' The argument, even yet, seems to me flawless, provided the miraculous premises are admitted. Before the end of the session, miracles had lost their interest for me, and the legal and vindictive creed in which I had been nurtured had passed away, like a cloud. I wanted to shorten the creed so that it should consist of one article only: 'I believe in a God who is omnipotent love, and I dedicate myself to His service'.

When the fact is recalled that those who enter the ministry of the Scottish Churches must take moral philosophy, as one of their subjects in the university, it becomes more easy to recognize than it is to measure the extent of Edward Caird's influence upon the ethical and religious beliefs of his time. But I must return to my personal story.

Caird once a fortnight gave his class three or four subjects on each of which they were expected to write brief exercises — unless they wrote the optional essays prescribed once a month and involving much more advanced work. He waded through and made notes on one half of these class exercises every fortnight — an immense amount of trying work — and returned the other half un-read. Amongst the first set he read was my class exercise, and it happened to be one of the best sent in. I was called up to read one of the exercises in the 'second-hour' meeting of the class. My success was wholly unexpected by me, and I was intoxicated with joy. And, there and then, I resolved to write the 'Optional Essays,' which meant competing with my fellow students for the Class Honours. My first essay, which was the first English essay I ever wrote, ranked third in the first class; my second essay, if I remember rightly, stood higher; and before long it became evident that another student and myself were decisively ahead of the rest of the class. Recognizing this fact and seeing him one day in the Reading Room which was then attached to the University Library, I went up to him and proposed that, in order to make the race fair, we should exchange the books that bore upon the subject of the essay at half-time. Till that moment we had been strangers; from that moment we were life-long friends. He accepted the proposal at once; and the competition bound us to each other even more closely. He was Mr. Hugh Walker of Kilbirnie.* At the close of the session the class would fain have divided the first prize between us, for the result of the year's work seemed to put us on a par; but, it being a medal, that method was not practicable, and by the majority of the votes of his fellow students the medal was

---

*Now Professor of English Literature, St. David's College, Lampeter.

awarded to Mr. Walker. I almost think that Mr. Walker would have preferred a different result. At any rate, as we walked together up to the college on the morning of the vote we settled the matter between ourselves by each of us expressing his conviction of the other's superior claims. There never was more honourable or more friendly rivalry for what we deemed a great honour, and many unexpected consequences followed it.

I passed the second part of the examination for the degree of M.A., namely the mathematical and physical, at the close of this session. There remained for the third and last session, the classes of logic and of English literature.

Inasmuch as I had attended the moral philosophy class already, under the guidance of Caird and also under his inspiring influence, while to all the other members of the logic class every branch of philosophy was strange and new, I expected that my pre-eminence would be obvious and convincing. It was not. The result of each of the three essays prescribed found me second to some person — a different person, by the by, each time. On my way up to college on the last day of the session, one of my fellow students told me that the class had resolved to award the class medal to me. (He was an Australian, I remember, and called Robert Hay.) Remonstrance was useless. The voting began as soon as the opening prayer was over; and it soon became evident that what Mr Hay told me was true. But I stood up in my place and said to the professor, 'Judging by the results given by you, sir, I do not deserve the medal, and I cannot accept it even if the majority of votes are for me'. The professor acquiesced; and the same process was repeated over the second prize. When the students were voting me the third prize, the professor himself interfered, and, not without anger, he refused the prize on my behalf. But I said that it accorded with his view of the value of my work, and that I would accept the prize if my fellow-students awarded it to me by their votes. They did so with cordial unanimity.

Apart from this incident I have no very living memories of the logic class. But no student can quite forget the length and unction of the opening prayer, the heat of the professor's wrath against Hegel and 'his meaningless jargon,' and the reading of the ballad of *Sir Patrick Spens*. Except for that ballad,

> The cloud-capp'd towers, the gorgeous palaces,
> The solemn temples

of the rhetoric which had its place in the class side by side with logic and psychology, have faded, leaving 'not a rack behind'.

It was far otherwise with the English literature class as taught by John Nichol. Once more I listened to a very great teacher, and became for the first time one of the heirs to a very great inheritance. Nichol revealed to me, and to others, the vast riches of our literature and made us ever afterwards lovers of it. There met in him qualities rarely found together but calculated to fit him for his work in a supreme way. In the first place, I believe he was the best public reader of both poetry and prose that I ever heard. In the next place he was most catholic in his tastes: recognized the literary value both of form and matter: every kind of literary excellence appealed to him, and he aired no aesthetic prejudices and obstinacies. More over his eloquence in class was at times' sweeping' in its power, for he threw himself unrestrainedly into his lectures, and, to crown all, I believe he was the most chivalrous man I have ever met. Misery always found in him, whether deserved or not, a fiery defence, as well as pity and help.

While still a student in his class I was more than once a guest at his table. I met Swinburne there once and watched him rolling in his chair as he recited one of his poems to us. Even yet I can hear Mrs. Nichol, whose soul was the very spirit of peace, restrain her husband's extravagances with the gentlest 'John! John!'; and I can see him yield at once. It was a delightful home to know.

John Nichol and Edward Caird differed from one another in every way; but they were, ever since the days of the 'Old Mortality Club' in Oxford, very intimate friends. One or two incidents illustrate at once the character of both of them, and will be my excuse for citing them. The first was told me by Edward Caird.

Lushington after his retirement as professor was made Lord Rector, and, as a very old man, was delivering his Rectorial Address in the Bute Hall. The students in the galleries could not hear him, and after a little while they occupied themselves otherwise than by trying to hear him. Nichol and Caird were standing together as keepers of order; and Nichol succeeded after several attempts in breaking away from Caird to take his place amongst a specially noisy group of students who were shooting peas at the audience. 'Nichol went to look after the students,' said Caird, 'and I went to look after him'. The students stopped shooting the peas; but one of them, provokingly mischievous, munched the peas off his palm. 'Look at that insolent fellow,' says Nichol to Caird. 'He does that just to annoy us.' 'Never mind him', was the most characteristic reply, 'you can't interfere with his eating his own peas!' But Nichol broke away again and said to the student, 'Sir! you should have brought thistles!' There was a roar of laughter which arrested the attention of the whole audience.

The other incident brings to light an aspect of Caird's character not always recognized by those who thought they knew him. He was very much more shrewd and observant of the character of the men and women he met than was usually thought. In other words he was less entirely up in the clouds. On this occasion I met Mr. Caird in Hillhead Street, and he turned me round to walk with him. 'I am going to see Nichol', he said, 'and to quarrel with him'. 'Surely', I replied, 'that is a very strange errand for you' — for I saw he was in earnest. 'It is the only way', said Caird. 'For a long time Nichol has been most difficult both to me and my brother' — the Principal. 'I shall provoke Nichol', he continued, 'and in his anger he will say such extraordinary things that he will be charming for many months'. I remember on one occasion saying to Mr. Caird, 'How can you put up with so many interruptions?' 'I leave a margin for them', was his wise and patient answer. And there were many other things for which he left a margin, amongst them the tempestuous extravagances of his great friend, John Nichol.

Soon after the close of the session I received a letter from Professor Nichol which had a decisive influence on my career. In that letter he told me that if I did not hurry into professional life, something might come of me.

I had undertaken the pastoral care of a Calvinistic Methodist chapel at Dolwyddelen, near Llanrwst; and it is just possible that Professor Nichol had heard that I was entering the sacred profession. His letter precipitated a notion I had been playing with into a sudden resolve. I gave up the chapel, and went to Bonn on the Rhine with my friend Hugh Walker, in order that we might continue our studies in philosophy and sit for honours in the following autumn. On our way to Germany we went to Wales, and, as a matter of course, I visited the great friend of my youth, Mrs. Roxburgh, now living in Bettws-y-Coed, and took Walker with me. Miss Roxburgh was there, a young lady a few years younger than Walker; and she made the evening most pleasant for us. Walker fell in love with her there and then, and irremediably. It was the only obvious case of boundless 'love at first sight' that I had ever witnessed. Although he was endowed with all the self-contained taciturnity of a Scotsman, not many days passed before he had made me his confession — of which, in fact, there was no need, for there were other evidences in plenty. One of the results was that I found myself committed to the most impossible task I ever faced. We were in Germany by this time: and I tried to teach Walker the first few notes of the song of Burns: —

> Of a' the airts the wind can blaw
> I dearly like the West, *etc.*

In all respects save one there was infinite variety in Walker's rendering of the song as he walked along the banks of the Rhine: somehow every note was out of tune.

Walker and I had a very happy and industrious summer in Bonn. We stayed with an old ivory-carver, in Struve Strasse, who had two fair daughters in the little shop he kept, and to whom he owed most of his trade with the university students.

With the help of these two young women Walker and I managed to witness a series of sword-fights between the students of the university. These were fought on that occasion in a kind of out-house, some two miles from the city; and an uncommonly silly and objectionable performance we thought it was. Five duels were fought that afternoon, and one man was seriously wounded.

On another occasion Walker and I had a most pleasant excursion on horseback up the Rhine; and on still another we held a feast in the Club of which we had been made temporary members, where the wines were very good and very cheap. When the hour became late, Walker and I might be heard alternately praising our respective mothers, and when the Club was closing we had a memorable walk together in the moonlight and amongst the fire-flies, along the left bank of the Rhine. The feast was intended to celebrate our finishing of the reading of Caird's *Philosophy of Kant*, and was to have been the first of a series. It remained the only one.

At the close of the summer Walker, who was well off, tempted me to spend my last penny on a Swiss tour. I thought the chance was not likely to come again in the way of Methodist preacher and I went. We sailed together up the Rhine, then went to Basle, and Lucerne, and over the St. Gothard to the Italian side. We descended to Airolo most expeditiously, for we sat on the green turf of the mountain side and slid down, amongst the grasshoppers, with great enjoyment. But we discovered afterwards that we had put our trousers to uses for which they were not intended. The last sight I saw for some nights after that adventure was Walker sewing deftly with his left hand, trying to repair and fortify himself behind. Having returned over the St. Gothard, we crossed the Furka Pass, saw the source of the Rhone and followed its course, walked up the glen to Zermatt, and down again during a wonderful thunder-storm. Then we went to Chamonix for a few days and took some of the well-known climbs, but not Mont Blanc itself. Thence we returned by Geneva, Lausanne, and Berne, and down the Rhine.

I arrived home penniless, having spent the last of the savings I had made while a schoolmaster. Then, I borrowed two pounds from Mrs. Roxburgh, to pay my fare to Glasgow and maintain myself pending the arrival of the instalment of Dr. Williams's scholarship, which the trustees, being pleased with my undergraduate course, had extended for a fourth year.

There was an interval of a few weeks before the degree examinations began, and this I spent in severe study. In the meantime the City of Glasgow Bank had come down, and Walker, with his mother and one of his sisters, was a share-holder.

This event brought so much confusion and so many responsibilities upon Walker — for his father was dead and he was the eldest son — that all thoughts of the examination so far as it concerned him were put on one side. Meantime I 'coached' with Mr. Patrick, Professor Veitch's assistant, who was already directing the studies of Thomas Kilpatrick and James Lambie.

The examination for the George A. Clark Fellowship in philosophy (which was awarded once every four years and was open to competition by graduates of four years' standing) took place in that autumn of 1878; and opinion was divided as to whether it would fall to Lambie or Kilpatrick. They were both senior as students by some years to me, and the best men of their time in their subject. The examination for the fellowship was the same as for honours: but I did not intend to compete for it. There were two other scholarships open and I had put in my name for each of these. But I called on Edward Caird, and having learnt that I had not put in my name for the Clark, he told me to do so — adding however, 'I do not say that you have any chance of winning it; but putting in your name will cost you nothing; and one never knows'. So I put in my name, and was thoroughly ashamed of having done so, as against Lambie and Kilpatrick.

One Sunday forenoon, Mungo MacCallum, then assisting Professor Nichol, afterwards a most admirable professor of English literature in Wales, and in Sydney, New South Wales, called on me in my lodgings at Willowbank Street, and took me to hear Lambie preaching in a neighbouring church. After the sermon, Lambie and MacCallum came back with me, and in the course of that afternoon (on whose suggestion I cannot now say) we resolved to found a philosophical society. This society was called *The Witenagemote* at the suggestion of MacCallum, whose humour was never asleep; and it had for many years a great influence on the study of philosophy in Glasgow. I was its first secretary. Its first meeting — the meeting, in fact, in which it was regularly founded, took place in a little public-house in Park Road, Hillhead, unless my memory deceives me. For at that time there was no Student's Union, nor any place within or connected with the university where students could meet for social purposes. The meeting took place between the examination for honours and scholarships in philosophy and the declaration of the results. Once business was over we indulged in university gossip; and, as a matter of course, the question was raised whether Lambie or Kilpatrick would be the winner of the 'George A. Clark.' Lambie insisted that it would be Kilpatrick, and Kilpatrick that it would be Lambie: but neither of them on being challenged to sell his chance would do so. Suddenly, in his thin, piping voice, MacCallum said to me, 'Jones! what will you sell your chance for?' I replied without a moment's

Henry Jones as a student at Glasgow.

hesitation 'Tuppence!' and the two pence were paid there and then.

Some days afterwards I called on Lambie. I had an overwhelming desire to withdraw my name from the honours examination, which it was possible for me to do so long as the results were not declared. I was certain I had only got a Second Class. No Welshman had ever got a First, and I set no value on anything less than a First. Lambie did his best to dissuade me. It was in vain, however: I went to withdraw my name. But on going up to the notice board I found that the results were already out! I had been given a First, and my cap went about as high as the college tower. I had no more care. I *knew* I had no chance for the Clark: I also knew that I would have another scholarship, for I was the only candidate for it.

Some days afterwards I was celebrating my success in gaining a First Class by having a fresh herring with my tea, when I received a message from Robert MacLehose asking me to go up to college and see who had won the Clark. He understood that the results were to be out that day. I went, and on my way up was congratulated on having won it myself; I got very angry, and told my informant that he had no right to make fun of me. He himself then 'huffed' also, and went his way. Then I ran a few steps, hoping; next I turned back, disbelieving; but finally I found myself in front of the board reading the announcement that the examiners had unanimously awarded the scholarship to me. It was 'the blue ribbon of the University,' said Mrs. Caird on congratulating me; and what was even more to the purpose it was at that time worth £225 a year for four years: a fortune for me. I do not believe in the least that I *ought* to have beaten either Lambie or Kilpatrick: they knew more than I did and had a firmer grasp. All the same I believe I did it; for I was better than myself in every examination.

The hard work, the excitement, the absence of the immediate need of any further strain — all these things combined, brought collapse. I needed rest, and I needed to be cared for; and I did not know it.

About this time, I visited Walker's charming home for the first time. There I found his noble old mother, and his three unmatched sisters and youngest brother. But it was not long before one of them was matched, for I proposed to the eldest of the three — a share holder in the bank — and I was accepted as a suitor, though the prospects of marriage were very distant. They did not come till April of 1882; and most persons would even then have doubted their arrival. But I persuaded my sweetheart that if I could not be a professor, I could be a minister; if I could not be a minister, I could be an elementary teacher, for I held the certificate; and if I could not get a school, I could make shoes. It seemed to us, in our optimistic mood, that I had more than the average strings to my bow.

But I must turn back to the winter of 1878–79. It was rather a barren winter, and I remember little about it. So, indeed, were all the four years during which I was Clark Scholar. I gave some assistance with the class examinations and essays to Edward Caird; I read some philosophy; I attended the meetings of the Witenagemote; I joined first the Free Church College and then the Established Church College as a divinity student and was as idle there as any of my fellows; and I formed some lasting friendships. Amongst the best of my friends were Professor Bruce and Dr. Marcus Dods who stood at my back on every occasion, and pardoned all my blatant heterodoxes. I also came to know Henry Drummond very well, and feel, as everyone did, the unrivalled charm of his character. He first taught me to observe the quiet colours in a natural scene, such as the colour of the soil of a ploughed field — where I had never thought of looking for beauty. But my closest friends were the Misses McArthur, who, in fact, mothered me. Miss Jane McArthur, I may say in passing, started and conducted for several years a series of correspondence classes for women. I was one of her tutors, Scotland knew no wiser or better friend to Women's Higher Education, then in its infancy, than Miss Jane was.

I cannot say how far my experience in Glasgow as a student was the same as that of others. But there was one feature in it which I still prize most highly and recall with gratitude and admiration. There could hardly be a youth in the university whose claims on the Glasgow citizen were lower than mine. I had no relatives there, but was a complete stranger and a Welshman: I had no social position, but was on the contrary quite poor. I never possessed a night-shirt! nor did I know that I ought to possess one. Far less had I an evening suit of swallow-tails. But this did not prevent Mr. Mirrlees, the head of a great firm of engineers, nor Mr. MacLehose, the university bookseller and publisher, from having me as their guest. On these occasions my fellow-lodger, Mr. McIntosh, whose brother-in-law I afterwards became, lent me his evening togs, and all went well. I should like to think that the Glasgow citizens who are well-to-do still take interest in some of the students of the university, who have no claims upon them, except their loneliness. I should deplore Glasgow's loss of its old generosities.

Walker and I went to Germany once more, and spent the summer of 1879 in Dresden. On this occasion Walker's younger brother, James, accompanied him and we also had with us James Denney, the best classical scholar of his time in the University of Glasgow, and afterwards the great Free Church leader. With Denney's guidance we renewed our studies of Greek and Latin and read Homer and Thucydides and Tacitus with very great enjoyment. Some of the afternoons we spent in the Art Gallery, but most of them in the Royal Garden then belonging to the city. And the four of us played the game of marbles in a secluded spot which we had discovered, until the German police came upon us and refused to let us play any more except in the children's *spiel-platz*, amongst the perambulators. Then we shifted our playground to the neighbourhood of the grave of Moreau, one of Napoleon's generals, some two miles out of the city. One way or another we had a profitable and happy time together in Dresden; and the friendship I then formed with Denney never grew old, nor was it in the least disturbed by any differences of view or outlook, whether theological or social, although the former were quite sufficiently decisive.

In the autumn of the same year, Walker and I went to Oxford: we intended to take a complete course of study and to graduate there, an intention which Walker fulfilled by taking his degree with a strong First in Greats. I passed the Preliminary and the Balliol Entrance examinations, and went no further. Three years as an undergraduate were more than I could face: I was nearly twenty-seven years of age, and the study of philosophy, which had won my soul, made it difficult for me to go back to conjugations and declensions and the minutize of scholarship which were unwisely made my exclusive diet. Instead of entering Balliol College I withdrew, and resolved to remain in Glasgow under the tutelage of Edward Caird and assisting him as Clark Scholar. I have no doubt that the decision was right. Whatever Oxford could have offered to me, to remain there as a student at that time would have done me more harm than good.

The years that followed, till the expiry of my scholarship in 1882, gave me opportunities for a fuller and more intimate knowledge of Edward Caird. There was hardly a week in which I might not be found in his study: and, even afterwards, when I was professor in Wales or in St. Andrews, or in Glasgow, there was, I believe, not one summer vacation a part of which we did not spend together. Either I went to him in the Lake District, or he and Mrs. Caird took a house near us in Wales, or stayed with us in Aviemore and Grenoble.

Perhaps the closeness and permanence of our friendly intercourse may justify me, before parting from him, to add to what I have already said of this great and good man — for he was certainly of a larger moral stature than any other man I have ever known. But these weightier and graver qualities were at once discernible to every one; and I have written of him elsewhere from this point of view.* Some of his other and lighter qualities, not so well known, may interest the reader. One of the most striking of these was his power to abstract himself from any person or object that was not in some way or another pleasing or profitable. 'How can you listen to such trashy sermons with patience?' I once said to him. 'I don't listen to them', was his reply, 'beyond a few sentences at the beginning, to find what the preacher would be at. After that, if I do not like his line of thought, I do not hear him at all.' The continued litigation over the publication of his class lectures by one of his students was naturally troubling and occupying his mind, especially when, as was then the case, it was before the House of Lords for final decision. But one afternoon, as we were starting for a walk in Wales, he said to me, 'I am not going to think of that matter any more.' I believe he literally kept his resolve. The case practically ceased to exist for him from that moment.

Another of his characteristics was his absent-mindedness. At times, especially when he was engaged upon his great work on Kant, he was

---

* See *Life and Philosophy of Edward Caird*, by Professor Muirhead and Sir Henry Jones.

apt to be quite oblivious of his surroundings. One day in Wales he left Mrs. Caird and myself on our walk in order to pay the formal parting visit to the local doctor. Mrs. Caird and I loitered long on the road, waiting for him; then she sent me to look for him. I found him sitting quite placidly in the surgery amongst the patients, chiefly babies on their mothers' arms. Another instance of absent-mindedness he related to me himself and I have always thought it very comical. 'I found myself', he said,'standing outside my bath, wondering whether I was coming out or going in!' And this was on a Glasgow winter morning!

I might multiply instances. 'Oh, Mr. Caird,' said the servant maid to him one day as he opened the front door of his house, 'you cannot go out like that!' He looked at the maid and she continued, 'Look at your trousers, sir!' He had been writing all the morning and a puppy dog had been playing about his feet; and it had chewed one leg of Mr. Caird's trousers up to the knee, without distracting his attention in the least.

A more charming guest I have never known. He would sit reading placidly for hours in the windy porch of the farm-house at Aviemore, while the children ran in and out, about his knees. But he was most helpless amongst them; and their mother trembled with fear when he tried to play with them. He was not able to join in their games at all or be one of them except in simplicity — nor could he answer their questions in their way. When my little daughter, Jeanie, sitting on his knee, pulled his whiskers and asked him 'why his hair grew there instead of on the top of his head,' he had not a word to say. One of his last visits to us was his visit to the old villa I had rented for the summer on one of the slopes about Grenoble. He was working at the time at his second series of Gifford Lectures, and I can even yet see him sitting peaceably, sheltering from the heat in our vine *tonnelle*, writing diligently all through the morning. That visit closed with a memorable drive over the Lautaret Pass, to the Italian side, through the noblest Swiss scenery.

So long as I was in Glasgow as Clark Scholar, our relation to one another was as much that of father and son as of teacher and disciple. He virtually reproved me once. It is true that his reproof took the form of advice, but it was advice that I knew I needed. 'Jones', he said, 'always keep your engagements'. Gentle as were his words, they were far too impressive to be forgotten; for his character was behind them. Engagements, whether great or small, acquired a new sacredness to me from that moment.

There was, however, one momentous engagement from which I sought release owing to his intervention. 'What is this you have been doing, Jones?' he said to me one evening, as he stood with his tall figure above the low chair when I sat in his study. I did not know what he meant, and was put about by his solemnity: so he continued. 'I hear that you have taken a church in Liverpool. Why! I intend you to be a professor of philosophy.' 'Do you, Mr. Caird?' I replied, jumping up in the joy of my heart; for somehow I had never dared to contemplate such a destiny. Not for a moment did I hesitate, or count the cost or probabilities of the new venture: the very first post carried to the officials of the church my resignation of the pastorate.

I had told Caird of my engagement to Miss Walker, and he was naturally desirous of meeting her. He happened to be ill and in his bed-room when I introduced them to each other, and very few words were said on either side. But there was one more instance of his saying what could not be forgotten: 'I look upon you two as my children'.

And so he did. My wife became first favourite with him 'at first leap'.

We were married on the 11th of April, 1882. My scholarship expired that year, and I had no other income. But, as I have already explained, I had a rich variety of prospects; and to young optimists, prospects can be helpful as well as luring, reliable as well as treacherous. Prudence, the prudence that will never leap, has always seemed to me the most ambiguous of all the virtues. In any case what with my prospects and somewhat sparse savings we honey-mooned in the Lake District, where, according to our Cockney landlord, 'the hair was very hembracin'!' Thence we went to Wales, and stayed for the summer at Llangernyw, near my father and mother. When autumn came we returned to Scotland and rented a cottage at Cambuslang; for Mr. Caird had invented an Assistantship for me, paying me, I need hardly say, out of his own pocket.

But before we had furnished the cottage, or I had begun my work

Lady Jones.

as Assistant to Caird, the world opened for us in a quite unexpected quarter. I was offered the Lectureship in Philosophy at the University College of Wales, Aberystwyth, at a salary, if I remember rightly, of £150 a year: and my services were to begin with the New Year.

We left Scotland; and it was not for nearly nine years that we returned there and I experienced anew the never-failing kindness of its people.

Chapter VI

The weather in Scotland about Christmas, 1882, was merciless: my wife was frozen out of her kitchen in Cambuslang. We found it sunny and kindly at Aberystwyth, — a place softened by the sea-air and, I believe, by the gulf-stream. A few days after our arrival my wife and I took a walk out into the country, and we found the red campion in full bloom in a wood. We adopted it on the spot as our family flower, and made it the symbol of our hopes. Since that time we have plucked it for one another more than once, when we were hard tried.

A more cheerful beginning of a new life could hardly be desired. I had arrived: for I had secured the two things which according to Hegel make life worth living: namely, the wife and the work which I loved. We took a house in Bryn-y-mor Road, within a few doors of my friend, Mungo MacCallum, then professor of English in the college. No outlook could be more auspicious. My class was small; but it was preparing for graduation in the University of London and one of its members was Mr., afterwards Sir Owen M. Edwards, a distinguished fellow of Lincoln College, Oxford and Chief Inspector of Schools for Wales. Besides this class I gave once a week a popular lecture on philosophy, which was very well attended, and appreciated in a way that was most encouraging to me.

But the halcyon weather did not last long. At the close of that term, my first, I found the post which I held advertised and candidates invited to apply for it; which meant, of course, that the college was dispensing finally with my services. I must explain the circumstances: but I do not propose to enter into any details. Instead, I shall put down the few facts necessary to make the situation intelligible, and ask the reader to draw any conclusions he pleases. It does not matter to me, and it does not matter to the dead.

1. There were at this time thirteen different towns competing for the university college to be founded somewhere in North Wales and

aided by a Government grant of £4,000 a year, conditional, however, upon local subscriptions.

2. Mainly by the efforts of William Rathbone, M.P. for North Carnarvonshire, a meeting was held at Chester, a committee was formed consisting of representatives of North Wales in either of the two houses of parliament and a resolution was passed in which the question of site was postponed to that of the subscriptions, a movement to obtain which was then and there inaugurated.

3. I was asked by the unanimous committee to be the secretary in charge of that movement; and, for that purpose, to obtain the permission of the Principal of my college to be absent for some six weeks, including the Easter holidays; while Mr. Rathbone undertook 'to pay handsomely for a substitute', lest my students should suffer by my absence.

4. The Principal, on my making the request, placed before me the following option. If I accepted the invitation to be the secretary of the North Wales movement, I ceased thereby to be a member of the college staff. In other words, I was dismissed. On the other hand, if I refused the invitation of Mr. Rathbone and the committee, my lectureship would be at once converted into a professorship, on the usual terms of tenure. I tried hard to shew that such an option need not be forced upon me. I believed that the Aberystwyth college would be moved into North Wales and gain by the movement. But my efforts, earnest as they were, failed altogether.

5. Bidden to approach the Principal for a second time, I was given the same option between what I thought my duty to my country and my means of making a livelihood. But, before that interview was over, *a complete change came over* the Principal's view. He gave me permission to accept the secretaryship, relieved Mr. Rathbone from the need of providing a substitute and undertook to do what was necessary himself. I had told him that I would let my countrymen know the option he had placed before me and all the circumstances.

6. My appointment as secretary was announced at once. Lord Aberdare, the president of the college, saw the announcement and cancelled the Principal's permission, on the ground that looked quite reasonable, namely, that the establishment of the North Wales college would be the death-blow of the college at Aberystwyth and that it

was not 'decent' that the death-blow should be delivered by a member of the staff.

7. The Parliamentary Committee gave way to Lord Aberdare and I took no part whatsoever in the movement for the North Wales college. Nevertheless, soon after the end of the term, I found that my post as lecturer at Aberystwyth was being advertised.

8. I desire it to be understood clearly that I *never resigned*. And the authorities of the college, instead of converting my lectureship into a chair, turned me off. It was from the public advertisement that I first learnt of my dismissal.

I was thus left, newly-married, without any visible means of earning a livelihood. But my wife and I were young, and cares did not bite. I cannot recall a single moment of monetary anxiety on the part of either of us. What I can recall is the drop in the temperature of the kindliness of my Aberystwyth neighbours — not that the closer friendships were in any way affected. I seemed then for the first time to find meaning in the Biblical phrases about 'a pelican in the wilderness' and 'a sparrow alone upon the house top', Psalm 102, 6, 7. Suspicions of my orthodoxy also spread like a contagion: and since those days I have often marvelled that I was not crushed. It is so easy for a person whom the public reveres to crush a young life at the beginning of its career. But 'let the dead bury their dead'.

Although I had no college duties, I had a busy summer; for Mr. Rathbone requested me to draw up the constitution of the new college, which was to be established at Bangor. This occupied me closely and privately for many weeks; and Mr. Rathbone gave me £50 for my work. The constitution, I may now say, was supposed to have been sketched by an episcopalian and was violently attacked for want of a satisfactory balance of sects, by the Liberal and nonconformist press. It is hardly necessary to say that I had tried a task in which no one has ever succeeded in Wales; namely that of 'being fair' as between the religious (?) sects.

The same summer found me appointed Examiner for Degrees in the University of Glasgow in the department of philosophy and English literature. The appointment lasted for three years, and carried a salary, I think, of £80 a year.

I was presiding, as invigilator, over the examination for degrees held at the close of the session when Edward Caird came up on the platform behind the students, where I sat, and placed a small book in my hand, asking me to look at it before he returned. It was called *Aids to Philosophy*, and, when Caird came back, I had no hesitation in saying to him that it consisted of garbled and unintelligent renderings of his own lectures. Asked if I would permit it to be published and sold, I answered with an emphatic 'No'. The students of the future would buy and use the book, and the result would be injustice to the subject and confusion of mind on the part of the student. The author pretended that the book was an independent production; Mr. Caird denied this, and asked for a legal injunction prohibiting its publication on the ground that it was, though confused and inaccurate, a pretended rendering of his own lectures. He sought to prove his conclusion by comparing the *Aids* with a previous, openly-professed, type-written copy of Caird's lectures, against the publication of which an injunction had already been obtained. For some weeks I was engaged in making this comparison and proving the affinity of the two productions; and, naturally, I was called as witness, and principal witness, in the case. I shall not follow its history further than by saying that it was won by Caird before the Sheriff, lost on appeal to the Edinburgh legal authorities, and won finally before the House of Lords. Until that time, the rights of a professor to publish his own lectures were not indisputably exclusive. Caird, as witness in a law court, was most impressive. He seemed to be eager to give his opponents the full rights of their contentions; but, having made every possible concession, there came a broadside from him that swept everything clean away. He was in very low spirits as we walked home together from the law court. But he managed, in his shy way, to ask me how he had done. 'You reminded me of Sam Weller, Mr. Caird', I said, 'You seemed to look round at the end and say — 'Is there any other gentleman who would like to ask me anything?" 'You rascal!' he replied: and the clouds lifted.

What with my prolonged visits to Scotland, the examinership and the litigation, the winter and spring of 1883–84 passed quite pleasantly, And my wife had a fuller and richer life than ever, for our eldest son was born in September, 1883.* Then came the election of

---

*Elias Henry Jones, M.A., author of *The Road to Endor*.

the Principal of the North Wales University College for which I was a candidate, backed by my Glasgow teachers and pupils and friends. In one sense, I had set my heart on the office; for, so far as I can judge, I can say without the least touch of exaggeration that I would have given my life for the well-being of the college. But before the election day had arrived, my hopes had been well chastened. The Calvinistic Methodist influence, inspired and sanctified by Principal Edwards and his father, ran against me like a powerful stream. And, in the second place, the scrutiny of my past life was too minute to leave one fleckless. My 'iniquities' were too well 'marked' to enable me 'to stand'. For instance, I was asked by a friend on the College Council if I could refute the charge made against me that I had 'smoked a cigar on the street at Porth Dinorwig on a Sunday afternoon!'

Fortunately both for the college and for me, the choice of the electors fell on Mr., now Sir Harry Reichel, a very distinguished Oxford scholar, and, I may add, after many years of close intimacy and friendship, an unselfish and judicious man — in whom trust grows from year to year as his character of a perfect gentleman reveals itself more and more.

I felt the disappointment deeply; but only for a few days. The deeper roots of my ambition had been unselfish and impersonal, and, as a consequence, healing came very quickly. Besides, I had still a chance of being elected as professor of philosophy in the college, and my prospects were quite hopeful. Only as the afternoon wore on and evening came, on the day of the election, did I know real anxiety. Matters did look somewhat dark as the hours lengthened without bringing any news; for the professorship was the last string of my bow that I genuinely valued. It appears that I was elected straightway when the Council met, and with the greatest cordiality, and that the meeting then passed on at once to the next business, the secretary forgetting both to inform the other candidate, Mr. Joseph Solomon, who was waiting in an adjoining room, and also to send a message to me! I entered on my work at Bangor with the opening of the winter session of 1884–85, and when I received the first moiety of my salary, we owed no man anything, and yet we had ten shillings in the bank. My wife and I had weathered the storm and come to port.

At that time and for some years afterwards the Welsh colleges prepared their students for the examinations of the University of London. There was no University of Wales. Philosophy did not enter into the curriculum of the candidates for the degree of B.A., till their final year, and even then only as an option. Students who preferred mathematics might go on with that subject and omit philosophy altogether.

A happy chance brought me during the first session two students who had passed their 'First B.A.', and were taking philosophy for one of their final subjects. They were both preparing for the ministry of the Baptist Church. One of them, Mr. John Thomas, had been a working miner. He passed the degree examination in philosophy at the head of the year's list after a bare twelve months' study and he took the M.A. degree afterwards in the same subject. He was afterwards appointed minister of an important Baptist chapel in Liverpool, and became one of the best known preachers of his day. The second student was Mr. Silas Morris. He has for many years been the trusted and esteemed Principal of the College in Bangor for training ministers of the Baptist Church. I was much less fortunate during the second session, so far as the inner work of the college was concerned. I had still two students, but neither of them was bright. The intellectual light of one of them was a very weak jet; and teaching left him uninformed and happy, and me helpless and despairing. The simplest logical deduction and the most well-worn was beyond his reach. Do what I would, I could not get him to see that one might not conclude that 'all animals are men' from 'all men are animals'. My outlook as professor was not bright. The best students naturally chose to go on with mathematics, a subject of which they knew something already, rather than to take up a new subject the nature of which no definition could make quite plain. It looked as if I could never be of much value to the college; and I found the consciousness of being of little use very heavy to bear. During that winter I had thoughts of resigning, and of seeking my livelihood elsewhere than in Wales. The temptation was strengthened by other facts: amongst them one which I still remember, not without resentment. The professors, and I believe Reichel, the Principal, also, delivered courses of extension lectures in the larger towns of North Wales. Naturally and rightly, all reasonable means were used in order to secure the success of these courses: on that success depended in great part that of the college itself. But I found myself one evening in a neighbouring town, whither I had been sent to deliver a series of extension lectures, expected by no one. The lectures had not been advertised anywhere, nobody knew anything about them, and, needless to say, no hall or meeting place of any kind had been secured. I felt silly and helpless, and not a little indignant. I thought that I was able, without any extraneous help, to secure my failures.

How this misadventure came about I never enquired, and I do not know. Even if the course I was to give was only overlooked and forgotten, there remains the plain fact that its success had not been an object of care to anyone. I believe that it was thought best at the time by good friends of the college, and even of myself, that the little candle I carried about lit in Wales should be kept under a bushel. Other lights would shine the more triumphantly. I need hardly say that the Principal himself knew and suspected nothing — he has neither faith in devious paths to good ends, nor the capacity to follow them. However, all this came to an end when, encouraged by Edward Caird, I spoke out and showed that my endurance had come to an end. After the storm broke, there was clear air; and I did not resign.

Instead of resigning, I thought I would try to let a few of the best students know what kind of diet I could offer them in philosophy. So I invited a number of young men, most of whom were about to become ministers, to meet me on Saturday mornings, and read John Caird's *Introduction to the Philosophy of Religion*. Amongst these, I remember, were the Rev. Professor John Owen Jones* and Professor Edward Edwards.† The experiment succeeded. All these men took philosophy for their final B.A. I had found my footing in the college and had no more anxiety of that kind. Meantime, educational affairs beyond the College became interesting, and were ultimately of great significance. One evening, during the first or the second college session, I was dining at Treborth, as the guest of Mr. Richard Davies, M.P. for Anglesey. On the opposite side of the table sat my friend, Mr.

---

*Late of the Preparatory School, Bala.
†Professor of History, University College of Wales, Aberystwyth.

Wm. Rathbone, M.P., who told me that he was going to speak for Mr. Davies on the morrow at Llangefni. I asked him if he would not speak about the Intermediate Education Bill which was being held back from year to year, in spite of the powerful case made by Lord Aberdare's Commission. Mr. Rathbone replied, 'How can I? Your Welsh members are afraid of the Bill. It contains a provision for a penny on the rates for the support of the schools; and they say that the very notion of an increased rate will infuriate their constituents.' I was thoroughly indignant, and vehemently assured Mr. Rathbone that, if the option between no rate and no schools on the one side and both the rate and the schools on the other were placed before my countrymen, they would decisively choose the latter. Mr. Rathbone was not hard to persuade. He was tempted to put aside the speech he had already prepared, and he took me for a further talk to a private room; then, late at night, he dismissed me, saying, 'Well! I'll see if what you say is true. Go home! I am going to prepare another speech.'

A day or two afterwards I found Mr. Rathbone excitedly calling for me at the foot of the stairs, in the Old College. As soon as he saw me, both his hands went up into the air and he cried, 'You were quite right, Jones! I put the matter before the audience at Llangefni and the vote for the schools and the rate was unanimous. And now', he added, 'you must organize! and we shall get the Bill read a second time, late as the session is'.

The task of organizing, at my request, was put in much more competent and experienced hands than mine. Mr. Cadwaladr Davies, Secretary of the College, took the matter up, and in a very few weeks meetings were held in the towns of North Wales calling for the Bill and accepting the rate. At the same time, Mr. R. A. Jones, barrister-at-law at Liverpool, one of the most enthusiastic friends the University College ever had, might have been seen, bareheaded, rushing from one place to another in Anglesey (where he had much influence), and persuading the little School Boards to meet and pass resolutions and send them up to their member, accepting the rate and demanding the Bill.

I addressed meetings at Llanberis, Blaenau Festiniog, and elsewhere, and on no single occasion was a single hand raised against the rating provisions of the Bill. But the meeting for the purposes of the Bill at Bangor brought another interesting event into my life, which I can hardly pass by in silence, for it made me once more take my professional existence in my hands. In the course of his speech, Reichel gave away his own right and that of his staff to take any public side in party politics. 'Neither I nor my colleagues would be here', he said, 'were this a political question'. One of my Scotch colleagues, on hearing this, whispered gruffly in my ear, 'Jones! you are to speak. If you do not contradict that statement, I shall ask the chairman's permission to speak, and do it myself.' I was nothing loath: and made it quite clear to the audience that in becoming professors of the college we had given up none of the rights of good citizens: and expressed the hope that some day I would be addressing them on a political question from that platform: I did not know if we, the professors, were more competent to judge of political matters than the tailors and shoe-makers of the town: but we had had the opportunities of a better education, and more might justly be expected and demanded of us when the good of the country was at stake.

After the meeting was over, the Principal and I walked together to Upper Bangor and discussed our difference. His view was that the conditions under which the college was starting on its way were such that for the staff to take a side in questions of party politics would be to imperil its existence. I maintained that, if we did not claim our freedom at the beginning and go our own way with little regard to ignorant public opinion, we should never be free men nor worthy to be teachers of youth or leaders of the community. The discussion, which was perfectly friendly as well as frank throughout, closed with Reichel's saying that, in his view, the college would dismiss the professor who took a public part in a political struggle; and in my replying that I would bring that matter to a practical test on the first occasion that offered.

As it happened the first occasion arose not long afterwards. I was invited to speak during a parliamentary election by Mr. Richard Davies, in Anglesey. Now, Mr. Davies was one of the two Vice-Presidents of the College, and the very last man that anyone would accuse of imprudence or hasty action of any kind. It was evident that I could not make a political speech under safer auspices; and I

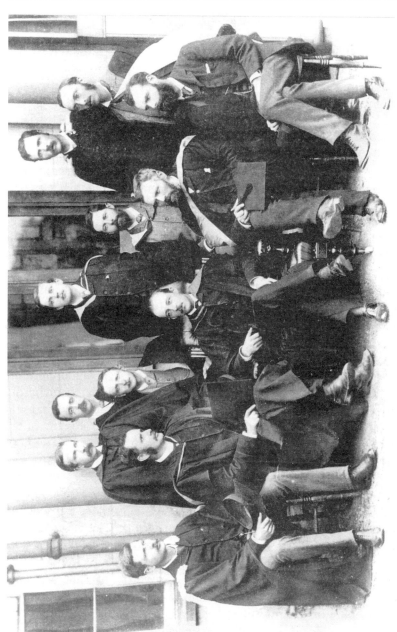

The original professorial staff of the University College of North Wales, Bangor, with Principal Reichel. Professor Henry Jones is seated second from the left. [University of Wales, Bangor Archive, copy by Eryl Rothwell Hughes]

promised to go. Mr. Rathbone heard of the matter and wrote at once to Mr. Davies saying, 'It would never do!' Mr. Davies sent on the message to me, but the matter had a personal side of which Mr. Davies knew nothing, and I refused to give up the engagement. I went and spoke, and spoke with the more earnestness, and probable effect, because I knew the personal consequences that might follow. It was at Llanerchymedd; and the audience was most enthusiastic. Then I spoke again for Mr. Davies at Beaumaris — a poor speech and a poor audience.

By this time the local conservative press had taken the matter in hand, and it appeared that it had at its command some vigorous language to spend on me. Concurrently with the attacks of the newspapers came the private, personal pressure of Mr. Cadwaladr Davies, the Secretary of the College, himself a well-known Liberal and sharing my views. He agreed with the Principal as to the risk to the college and also as to the obligations of the college staff under those early circumstances. I replied that my Scottish colleagues, at least, and possibly others, took my view of the situation and that, if I was dismissed, they would resign. In short, I refused to give way. Mr. Davies then, expert man as he always was, took a different line of action. He told those who were responsible for the attacks upon me to let me be, lest worse should follow; and he so exaggerated the political influence I might exert that I was let alone. It is hardly necessary to add that nothing followed. No attention of any kind was paid to the question, so far as I ever heard: and the professors of the University College of North Wales were permitted to enjoy, without any question, the ordinary rights of the ordinary citizen.

The Intermediate Education Act was passed in 1889, and immediately afterwards Mr. Arthur Acland, M.P., invited a few men known to be interested in the subject to his house at Clynnog, to meet Mr. Thomas Ellis, M.P., and to discuss the clauses of the Act. It was a most interesting group that met, and every member of it was keen to discover and make the best use of the possibilities of the Act. The group included the Rev. Professor Ellis Edwards, of Bala, Mr. John Powell, of Wrexham, Mr. R. A. Jones, of Liverpool, Mr. Cadwaladr Davies, of Bangor, and myself.

Two different and mutually inconsistent lines of policy were advocated at this time in Wales by well-meaning and well-informed men. One party desired to establish a small number of schools — say, about one in each county, and to equip these thoroughly. The other party, believing that to bring the opportunities of education within the reach of the people was of vital importance, thought there ought to be an Intermediate School in every natural centre of rural life. I was of the latter opinion. 'Bring the opportunities of mental as well as physical health and growth home to the people.' I remember saying in a speech in an Anglesey village, 'One school for Anglesey!! I would as soon have one oven for baking the bread.' The illustration was the more telling in that every smallest village, and every little cottage that stood aloof by itself, had its own oven.

All of us who met at Clynnog took this same view. It involved the building of a very large number of new schools, and their maintenance afterwards. We indicated the places in which we believed the schools in the northern counties of Wales should be placed by sticking pins into a map; and before we had done the map was bristling with them. We were well aware that we were indulging ourselves in constructing a scheme that was ideal: I do not think any one of us believed it to be attainable. But some few years after this time, I was addressing the closing meeting of the County School at Carnarvon, and I told the audience about that meeting of the educational enthusiasts at Clynnog. I had to add, however, and I did so with exceeding great pride and gratitude, that we had not stuck enough pins in the map! We had underestimated the strength of the national impulse for higher education. It was the more marvellous in that the national movement for the establishment of the schools came immediately after the founding of the colleges.

The results of our deliberations at Clynnog were gathered into a little volume by our hosts, Mr. Arthur Acland, and Mr. Thomas Ellis. We aimed at guiding public opinion on the matter; and there was one adventitious circumstance which proved of considerable help. Our host was an influential member of the Carnarvonshire County Council. He led that Council, for he was the only person who knew the powers conferred by the Act: and he got it to move at once. In this way Carnarvonshire quietly gave the lead to the other counties, and the whole of North Wales moved along the lines which we had sketched at our little gathering. Of course we employed other means also. Mr. Thomas Ellis never lost an opportunity of supporting the good cause by his public speeches and otherwise, and other members of our group did the same. I advocated our scheme and pressed the cause home as well as I could in the public press: for several weeks a series of letters which I wrote appeared in seven Welsh and eight English newspapers. All through the winter Mr. Cadwaladr Davies and I went together, authorized by no one, at our own expense, and thanked by no one, and held meetings every week in which we pleaded for the establishment of the schools. Some of these meetings were well attended and enthusiastic; others were in every respect the opposite. I remember once looking through the window before entering a place of meeting and saying to Cadwaladr Davies 'Myn gafr! 'does yma neb'. ('By the goat, there isn't a single person here.') I was wrong. Before the meeting closed, there were several persons present. Perhaps I should add, however, that this was the nadir of our experience.

Above all, I should like to say that, in the meantime, while this struggle was going on and prospering in North Wales, Principal Viriamu Jones was maintaining the same cause in South Wales, and, literally, giving his life for it.

It was a wonderful movement, and to witness it was a privilege. Wales proved itself capable of being stirred by a noble purpose — which is about the best thing one can say of either an individual or a nation. Technical obstacles were swept out of its course. Long before they were legally authorized, the County Councils in Wales, without a single exception, had committed themselves to the penny rate; and it was enacted so far as I can judge, by men who had as little formal authority as the tailors of Tooley Street — that the schools had to be provided free by the localities where they were placed, and built on free-hold ground.

Perhaps it will interest the reader to be given a concrete example of this national movement, which, so far as I know, stands to this day unique and without a rival. The most interesting in my experience was the struggle for continuing the little 'higher' school, established about 300 years ago by a good bishop, at Bottwnog in the Lleyn Peninsula. I was on holiday at the time with my family at Abersoch;

and I took part in the struggle on the challenge of the Bishop of St. Davids,* then Dean of St. Asaph, who had attended the school as a lad.

A meeting was held at (I think it was) Llanengan, Bishop Owen's native village, and addressed by him and others. During its course I discovered that the audience had a wrong impression of the conditions under which the Bottwnog School could be continued. They thought that it might remain in the future, what it had been in the past, a Church of England school. I explained that this was impossible. Either the school would be an Intermediate School under the national scheme like others, or else it would be closed and the funds would be used as scholarships for the brighter Bottwnog boys, or in order to improve the equipment of the new school at Pwllheli. The first result of my interference was that I scared away the support of the episcopalians and land-owners. The donations which had been promised, and which amounted to some £700, were withdrawn. But it was not the only result. The support of the people of Lleyn, which on the whole is chapel-going, was gained, and, as time went on, made more and more secure and full. The last stage of the struggle was delightful to witness and is worth recording.

I received a telegram one morning asking me to meet Mr. Thomas Ellis, M.P., at Sarn, and go with him to Aberdaron — an interesting old village at the very point of the Lleyn Peninsula, supposed to have retained more aboriginal Welsh features, and to be in that respect more interesting, than any other place. The policy of Mr. Ellis, who had decisive influence, was to close the school at Bottwnog and use the funds at Pwllheli. But when he reached Sarn he found a number of dripping-wet farmers waiting for him, ready to expound their rival plan. I had summoned them *in his name, and he knew nothing about it;* and they had come through the pouring rain. I wished him to hear the rural voice pleading for the little school; for I thought I knew the way to his heart. Mr. Ellis gave his arguments, every one of them sound, in support of the view he had formed, and made it quite clear in what ways the best boys of Bottwnog would benefit from the bigger and

---

* Rt. Rev. John Owen.

better equipped school at Pwllheli. But his contentions were countered one by one by the homespun arguments of the farmers. They held that, if the scholarships would be valuable, the comparative expenses of upkeep at Pwllheli would be heavy. The boys would want finer clothes, and play at cricket and things; and instead of *shot* or *bara-llaeth* they would want mutton-chops and puddings. 'No, Mr. Ellis, let us have our boys in their ribbed breeks (trwsus rhesog) which their mothers can patch, and let them play about our own fields, and live on bread and milk; and let us keep our little school; and let Pwllheli look after itself.' It was evident that now and then, Mr. Ellis was touched by their simple earnestness, well-mixed, as it was, with homely shrewdness. He had not the heart to hold his own against them.

It was late in the afternoon when the interview came to an end, and Mr. Ellis started for Aberdaron with his friend, Mr. D. R. Daniel. I went with them a part of the way; but I had to address a meeting on behalf of the school that evening, at Sarn, and a memorable meeting it was for its enthusiastic unanimity. It was some years before I heard the end of the Bottwnog visit of that splendid Welshman, Mr. Tom Ellis; for, before that year was out, I had left Wales for Scotland. It appears that Mr. Ellis did not go to Aberdaron, after all; it was too late. He turned back, and went about through the village of Bottwnog, and had a look at the little school, and strolled round the little fields which belonged to it, and peered in through the windows. And then he said, raising his fist, 'They shall *not* close this little school.' Nor was it closed.

After a brief interval, during which Mr. Ellis had been active, I received a hint which I at once conveyed to the farmers that, provided the local subscriptions were sufficiently large, the school would be continued. The result was wonderful. The Lleyn Peninsula and two successive market days at the delightful old town of Pwllheli were seething with Intermediate Education and the defence of the Bottwnog School. About the close of that memorable fortnight, I met a committee which was in charge of the movement at Bottwnog. I found its members there and then binding themselves legally to be responsible for £1,200 in support of the school. And I shall never forget the two way-weary men, who had walked through the heat all the way from Aberdaron, as they entered the meeting late, looking as shy and guilty as if they had been stealing sheep. They had sought, and, I believe, received subscriptions in every house in Aberdaron, the subscriptions varying from two pence to ten pounds. The memory of that Bottwnog movement still gives me joyous pride — the common people of Wales proved so much above the common.

But I must return to my proper sphere and work, which were those of a professor in a young college that was gradually and securely gaining the good-will and confidence of the community. There was something of a storm in its first days. Some members of the Council wished its meetings to be open, and representatives of the press to be allowed to attend its sittings and make a public record of its proceedings. Reichel held resolute views against the proposal, and would probably have resigned, had it been carried. But it was rejected, and all went well. The staff was on the side of the Principal in this matter and the Council acquiesced, and the relations between them were, what they have been since, thoroughly harmonious and happy. Naturally there was no lack of opportunity for differences of opinion, and the different academical experiences of the members of the staff, heirs, as they were, of the traditions of Oxford, Cambridge, and Scotland suggested to them different directions which the college might take. But neither was there any lack of opportunity for discussing these differences, and doing so informally, in our little social gatherings and very often at the Principal's dinner-table. Happy little dining-parties naturally generate agreement and sometimes wisdom as well. At any rate the first group of professors at Bangor College, which, I understand, now goes by the name of 'the old guard,' moved together harmoniously, and the college was founded mainly on Scottish lines. Its academic aims were always high; it sought public favour only by the excellence of the work it did; and it maintained at their true level the best ideals of collegiate life. As the years passed the college developed securely and peaceably, and its peaceful prosperity left no historical foot prints. The students increased in number; more subjects were added to the curriculum and taught, and new lecturers and professors were appointed.

Nor is there anything of importance or interest to record about myself during these years. The number of students taking my own subject was quite satisfactory, and the place of philosophy was quite safe. Nor were there any mishaps in the degree examinations, for, during the seven years of my professorship at Bangor, I believe none of my students failed. And I had a most happy home. We had moved from Upper Bangor two miles into the country; and we lived in the front portion of a large farm-house, most appropriately called Perfeddgoed. My wife lost her heart to it, when she saw the grass plot in front of the house surrounded by snowdrops, and her love and longing for it deepened, when, later in the season, she rambled in the wood at the back of the house and saw the very atmosphere tinged with the blue of the hyacinths that grew in such plenty around the path. Two of our children were born there, and, with the three who were older, were nursed and played around their mother amidst the peace of the green fields and in hearing of the songs of the birds. In the mornings, my wife usually walked with me on the way to college, and the whole expanse of the Snowdon range, from Snowdon itself to the sea at Penmaenmawr, lay before her.

On Saturdays some of the students usually came up to Perfeddgoed and we played at quoits in one of the fields. Not infrequently, I preached on Sundays in one of the chapels of the Calvinistic Methodists. And, during one winter, I taught sol-fa one evening a week to a number of quarrymen and farmers' sons in the little chapel hard by Perfeddgoed. One of these *sol-fa* pupils became well known in Bangor and the neighbourhood through his rendering of the most preposterously braggart song — both tune and words — ever written. It was written for him, because it suited him; and he delighted in it, whether he sang it in one of the little local Eisteddfods, or in his own home: where he used to take his stand at successive steps of the staircase and ask from the different heights — 'How does it sound from here, father?' Richard Prichard, singing *The Elephant*, was a public benefactor of no mean worth.

My last vacation, while professor at the University College of North Wales, found me a very busy man. During the previous winter and spring, I had delivered lectures on Browning in Cambridge, amongst other places, to one of the societies of the university. A resolution was passed in a very cordial fashion, expressing a request that I should publish the lecture. I agreed to the request; and, as soon as vacation began, set about fulfilling it. But the lecture grew into a book under my hands, and, at first, more or less against my will. Ultimately the exigencies of competition for a professorship in Scotland made it desirable that the book should be published before the vacation ended.* In consequence I was most fully occupied. During good days I might have been seen writing, within the power of the passionate grip of Browning's poetry, under one of the noble elm trees at Perfeddgoed. The proofs were read at Abersoch, in the intervals of the Bottwnog campaign; and at the close of the vacation my book on Browning was published and soon afterwards I was elected Professor of Logic and English in the University of St. Andrews.

Sir Henry Jones was Professor of Logic and Rhetoric at the University of St. Andrews from 1891 to 1894. In 1894 he succeeded his former teacher, Edward Caird, as Professor of Moral Philosophy at the University of Glasgow, a position he held until his death. He was awarded the degree of Ll.D. by the University of St. Andrews in 1895, and the degree of D.Litt. by the University of Wales in 1905. In 1911 he received a knighthood. Early in 1922 he was made a Companion of Honour. He died at Tighnabruaich on the fourth of February 1922, and is buried at Kilbride.

Browning as a Philosophical and Religious Teacher. (Glasgow: MacLehose, 1891.)